Feminists Researching
Gendered Childhoods

Feminist Thought in Childhood Research

Series editors: Jayne Osgood and Veronica Pacini-Ketchabaw

Drawing on feminist scholarship, this boundary-pushing series explores the use of creative, experimental, new materialist and post-humanist research methodologies that address various aspects of childhood. *Feminist Thought in Childhood Research* foregrounds examples of research practices within feminist childhood studies that engage with post-humanism, science studies, affect theory, animal studies, new materialisms and other post-foundational perspectives that seek to decentre human experience. Books in the series offer lived examples of feminist research praxis and politics in childhood studies. The series includes authored and edited collections – from early career and established scholars – addressing past, present and future childhood research issues from a global context.

Feminists Researching Gendered Childhoods

Generative Entanglements

Edited by

Jayne Osgood and Kerry H. Robinson

BLOOMSBURY ACADEMIC

LONDON • NEW YORK • OXFORD • NEW DELHI • SYDNEY

BLOOMSBURY ACADEMIC
Bloomsbury Publishing Plc
50 Bedford Square, London, WC1B 3DP, UK
1385 Broadway, New York, NY 10018, USA

BLOOMSBURY, BLOOMSBURY ACADEMIC and the Diana logo are
trademarks of Bloomsbury Publishing Plc

First published in Great Britain 2019

A catalogue record for this book is available from the British Library.

A catalog record for this book is available from the Library of Congress.

ISBN: HB: 978-1-4742-8578-0
        ePDF: 978-1-4742-8580-3
        ePub: 978-1-4742-8579-7

Series: Feminist Thought in Childhood Research

Typeset by Integra Software Services Pvt. Ltd.
Printed and bound in Great Britain

To find out more about our authors and books visit www.bloomsbury.com
and sign up for our newsletters.

Dedication

Here's to strong women. May we know them. May we be them. May we raise them.
Unknown

Contents

List of Illustrations

Figures

Images

Photographs

Tables

Notes on Contributors

Jayne Osgood is Professor of Education at Middlesex University, UK; formerly Visiting Professor at the Western Sydney University, Australia; and currently Professor II at OsloMet University, Norway. Her present methodologies and research practices are framed by feminist new materialism. She was co-founding member of Performing Methodologies in Early Years Education Research (PMEYER, with Professor Ann Merete Otterstad, OsloMet) and co-founder (with Professors Jessica Ringrose, Emma Renold and Anna Hickey-Moody) of the PhEMaterialism Network which seeks to advance feminist new materialist methodologies in educational research. Through her work she seeks to maintain a concern with issues of social justice and to critically engage with early childhood policy, curricular frameworks and pedagogical approaches. She has published extensively within the post-paradigm including special issues of the journal *Contemporary Issues in Early Childhood* (2006, 2016 and 2017, forthcoming) and *Narratives from the Nursery: Negotiating Professional Identities in Early Childhood* (2012). She is a member of several editorial boards, including *Contemporary Issues in Early Childhood* and *British Education Research Journal*, and is currently co-editor of *Gender & Education Journal* and *Reconceptualising Education Research Methodology*. She is also editor (with Veronica Pacini-Ketchabaw) of the *Feminist Thought in Childhood Research* book series for Bloomsbury, which includes this volume.

Kerry H. Robinson is Professor of Sociology in the School of Social Sciences and Psychology at the Western Sydney University, Australia. Her research interests include diversity and difference, gender and sexuality, gender and sexuality diversity, sexual and gender harassment/violence, constructions of childhood and sexuality, sexuality education and transformative pedagogies. She has published widely in her research areas, including a recent book, *Innocence, Knowledge and the Construction of Childhood: The Contradictory Relationship between Sexuality and Censorship in Children's Contemporary Lives* (2013), and a co-authored book, *Diversity and Difference in Early Childhood Education: Issues for Theory and Practice with Criss Jones-Diaz* (2017).

Mindy Blaise is Professor at Edith Cowan University, Australia. Before joining Edith Cowan University, Mindy was a kindergarten teacher in the United States. She has worked in American, Australian and Hong Kong universities. Her scholarship advances post-developmental and post-empirical approaches to reconfigure early childhood research, teaching and curriculum. By 'grappling-with' feminist practices, her work interrupts the notion of the developmental child. Mindy is a founding member and principal researcher of the Common World Childhoods Research Collective that promotes interdisciplinary research that focuses upon more-than-human childhood relations and pedagogies. Mindy publishes across both early childhood education and gender studies. Her book, *Playing It Straight! Uncovering Gender Discourses in an Early Childhood Classroom* (2005), brings together feminism, queer theory and early childhood to rethink childhood, teaching and learning. Her more recent book, *The SAGE Handbook of Play and Learning* (2014), was co-edited with Liz Brooker and Susan Edwards, and it showcases how post-developmentalism is taken up in early childhood.

Bronwyn Davies is an independent scholar based in Sydney, Australia. She is Professorial Fellow at the University of Melbourne, Australia. She was awarded an Honorary Doctorate for her work in early childhood at Uppsala University, Sweden. Her groundbreaking book from the late 1980s, *Frogs and Snails and Feminist Tales*, has been translated into Swedish, German and Spanish and the first chapter into Hindi. She has authored 17 books and more than 130 book chapters and papers, many of them co-authored. She visits England, Ireland, Belgium, Czechia, Sweden, Denmark, Finland, Norway and the United States to lecture, to assist PhD students and other scholars in their academic writing and to run research workshops. Over the last five years, she has published several books including *Listening to Children: Being and Becoming* (2014); a children's story *The Fairy Who Wouldn't Fly* (2014, by the National Library of Australia); *Deleuze and Collaborative Writing: An Immanent Plane of Composition* (2011), with Wyatt, Gale and Gannon; *Place Pedagogy Change* (2011), with Somerville, Power, Gannon and de Carteret; and *Pedagogical Encounters* (2009), co-edited with Gannon.

Debbie Epstein is Professor of Cultural Studies in Education (part-time) at the University of Roehampton, UK. She became an academic after a career in school teaching, gaining her PhD in 1991. Since then she has opened up several fields of investigation within educational sociology and has been at the forefront in their development. Specifically, her work in the early 1990s raised questions about sexualities in schools and was concerned to examine the normalization of heterosexuality. She has also worked on issues of whiteness and is a leading researcher on issues of masculinities in education and boys' 'underachievement'. Debbie has an international reputation for her research in the fields of cultural studies and sociology which addresses education and popular culture, specifically sexuality, race, masculinities and femininities. She has undertaken extensive empirical work in the UK and South Africa. Within education, her research spans different educational sites from early years to universities, while within popular culture, the primary focus has been on televisual cultures. Professor Epstein's work brings together a number of themes, including sexuality, gender and race; school cultures; the spread and prevention of HIV, particularly in Southern Africa; wider questions of media texts and audiences; and aspects of pedagogy in the formal and hidden curricula.

Jen Lyttleton-Smith is Research Associate for the Children's Social Care Research and Development Centre (CASCADE) in the Cardiff University School of Social Sciences, UK. CASCADE is concerned with all aspects of community-based responses to social need in children and families, including family support services, children in need services, child protection, looked-after children and adoption. Jen was awarded her PhD at Cardiff University, UK, in 2015. Her research explored the emergence of gender in preschool years based upon an ethnographic study conducted in a nursery with three- and four-year-olds. Her work engages with post-structuralist and new materialist perspectives, particularly the application of Karen Barad's agential-realist onto-epistemology to early childhood. She teaches at Cardiff University and acted as general secretary to the Gender and Education Association. She is also a member of the Gender and Sexualities Research Group at Cardiff University and co-founded the Young Sexualities Research Network.

Veronica Pacini-Ketchabaw is Professor of Early Childhood Education in the Faculty of Education at Western University, Canada. She is co-director of the Ontario Centre of Excellence in Early Years and Child Care and the British Columbia Early Childhood Pedagogies Network. Prior to joining Western University, Canada, Veronica was Professor at the School of Child and Youth Care at the University of Victoria, Canada, where she now serves as Adjunct Professor. Her writing and research contributes to *Common World Childhoods Research Collective* (tracing children's relations with places, materials and other species) and the Early Childhood Pedagogies Collaboratory (experimenting with the contours, conditions and complexities of twenty-first-century pedagogies). She is author/ co-author of more than thirty peer-reviewed articles and six books, including *The Common Worlds of Children and Animals: Relational Ethics for Entangled Lives* (forthcoming), *Encounters with Materials in Early Childhood Education* (2017), *Youth Work, Early Education, and Psychology: Liminal Encounters* (2016), *Unsettling the Colonial Places and Spaces of Early Childhood Education* (2015), *Journeys: Reconceptualizing Early Childhood Practices* (2014) and *Flows, Rhythms, and Intensities of Early Childhood Education Curriculum* (2010). Veronica is co-editor of the open access *Journal of Childhood Studies, Child & Youth Studies Dialogues* and the Bloomsbury book series *Feminist Thought in Childhood Research*.

Series Editors' Introduction

The series *Feminist Thought in Childhood Research* considers experimental and creative modes of researching and practising in childhood studies. Recognizing the complex neo-liberal landscape and worrisome spaces of coloniality in the twenty-first century, the *Feminist Thought in Childhood Research* books provide a forum for cross-disciplinary, interdisciplinary and transdisciplinary conversations in childhood studies that engage feminist decolonial, anticolonial, more-than-human, new materialisms, post-humanist and other post-foundational perspectives that seek to reconfigure human experience. The series offers lively examples of feminist research praxis and politics that invite childhood studies scholars, students and educators to engage in collectively to imagine childhood otherwise.

Until now, childhood studies has been decidedly a human matter focused on the needs of individual children (Taylor, 2013). In the Anthropocene (Colebrooke, 2012, 2013), however, other approaches to childhood that address the profound, human-induced ecological challenges facing our own and other species are emerging. As Taylor (2013) reminds us, if we are going to grapple with the socio-ecological challenges we face today, childhood studies need to pay attention to the *more*-than-human, to the *non*-human others that inhabit our worlds and the *in*human. Towards this end, *Feminist Thought in Childhood Research* challenges the humanist, linear, and moral narratives (Colebrook, 2013; Haraway, 2016) of much of childhood studies by engaging with feminisms. As a feminist series, the books explore the inheritances of how to live in the Anthropocene and think about it in ways that are in tension with the Anthropocene itself.

The inaugural book, *Feminists Researching Gendered Childhoods: Generative Entanglements*, introduces readers to the series by foregrounding feminist theories and practices within early childhood studies and by realizing its new materialist and post-humanist ambitions. Through theoretically rich and situated dialogues, the editors and authors address the convergences, continuities and gaps between feminist post-structural and feminist new materialist contributions to childhood studies. They carefully explore and debate the methodological dimensions of (so-called) 'new materialist feminisms' that have emerged in childhood studies in the past decades. Charting the evolving (and rhizomatic) nature of feminist theorizing and research methods in the field, as well as the generative potential they have for continually reconfiguring childhood and gender, the book attends to the important ways in which early childhood studies have shifted over time and with what effects and affects. Yet *Feminists Researching Gendered Childhoods: Generative Entanglements* does not only recognize the shifts. It also offers a celebration of the vital contributions that all waves of feminisms have made over the past three decades to advancing critical thought on gender and its intersections with other subjectivities (such as race, ethnicity, class, sexuality, disability, age, geographical location and so on) in childhood studies.

In the spirit of this series' aim to experiment, the editors of *Feminists Researching Gendered Childhoods* open the collection with a creative invitation to stay with the generative tensions and struggles that feminist theories contribute to childhood studies. They write:

This book might be engaged with diffractively; we invite readers to delve in and read chapters through each other or in isolation, in sequence or more haphazardly. The project we have set ourselves is transversal, not a linear chronology of where we once were as feminist researchers to where we are now. The aim is to illuminate the threads, connections, sticky knots and productive possibilities that come about from a project of this nature.

The chapters 'avoid the linear, progressive, Time's-(killing)-arrow mode of the Techno-Heroic' story, as Ursula Le Guin (1986: 153) so eloquently writes. It is this interruption to the heroic masculinist and dominant linear tale of early childhood studies that makes this book unapologetically feminist. As the editors note, 'the F-word' is central in the entire collection.

Through this critical engagement with feminisms, the book is also situated within post-developmental early childhood perspectives. Widely defined, post-developmentalism recognizes that children are differentially situated in terms of class, gender, 'race', sexuality, ethnicity, places of origin, abilities and other social positions. Post-developmentalism politicizes the 'truths' of early childhood studies and shifts developmental theories' dominant position as the lens through which 'the child' and 'childhood' are viewed. In other words, by exploring multiple feminist lenses and contexts, the post-developmental perspectives outlined in *Feminists Researching Gendered Childhoods* endeavour to disrupt child development as neutral knowledge. The authors disrupt and reframe gender outside of developmental psychology – which detrimentally have become normalized as the singular and natural way to shape discussions on gender in early childhood.

Preface

A Situated Reading of *Feminists Researching Gendered Childhoods*

Hillevi Lenz Taguchi

Introduction

Feminism has asked an intensely active question, *not* 'What does it mean?', *but* 'How does it work?' What can this concept or theory do? (Colebrook, 2000: 8)

It is an honour to be asked to write the preface to a book that foregrounds and permeates feminist scholarship and research in childhood studies. Such a foregrounding is unfortunately rare. This is peculiar. Childhood studies is predominately about the subjectivity of the child, and it is probably feminist scholarship that has done more than any other scholarship in the social sciences and humanities to understand what our sense of subjectivity *does* in our lives, to ourselves, and to the world of humans and more-than-humans around us. This is something that the scholars in the present volume creatively manage to contribute to, by making skilful and important transversal cuts through the theoretical, personal *and* political. Hereby, this collection of texts, analysis and interviews contributes considerably by giving some important new examples and analyses, as well as discussing the possibilities and difficulties of feminist childhood studies.

It is in relation to the above quote by Colebrook and in the spirit of Haraway's (1988) concept of a feminist *situated knowledge* – which constitutes a strong undercurrent in this volume – that I have made the choice to offer a situated reading in relation to some of the contents and arguments of this collection of texts. I have chosen to do so since this is exactly in line with what the authors of this book are themselves attempting to do. In the second chapter, Jayne Osgood and Kerry Robinson are historically situating feminist academic and activist work in an international Anglo-cultural context. What is described in this chapter has influenced feminist work all over the world and is something which researchers like myself have related to and drawn upon throughout our entire careers. In Chapter 3, the voices of interviewed feminist researchers from various Anglo-cultural contexts across the globe – Mindy Blaise and Bronwyn Davies from Australia, Veronica Pacini-Ketchabaw from Canada and Debbie Epstein and Jen Lyttleton-Smith from the UK – are diffractively interweaved as they describe their various entry points into and engagements with feminist post-structuralist and feminist new materialist and post-humanist theories. However, the reading I will be offering in this preface is made from what must be considered a marginal sociocultural context in relation to the Anglo-cultural contexts described in these chapters, although performed by a white, middle-class, heterosexual academic in a most privileged cultural context within the Swedish academy. It is, as Annemarie Mol notes, the only reading I – in honesty – can do. Mol (2008: 29) writes: 'Situating does not only have to do with where you are, but includes where you come from and where you may go.'

Currently, the abhorrent threats from populist and right-wing political movements in Sweden, as in the rest of Europe, need substantial critical attention from all of us. The present reading nonetheless evolves from and discusses a socio-historical situatedness where feminism and gender politics are not merely taken seriously but, in a number of social settings, constitute more or less taken-for-granted discursively informed material practices. These practices are foremost academic, scientific, educational and to the state and municipality administration. Although academic work is always *also* political, for me, doing academic work and research is still not the *same* as doing politics, or doing art, or being an activist, per se. Making this reading implies relating the texts of the present volume with the above quoted intense feminist question (Colebrook, 2000: 8): '*not* "What does it mean?"' because we all know – more or less – how shared concepts in international research which are presented in this volume are defined, '*but* "How does it work?" What can this [the] concept[s] or theor[ies of this book] do?' It is my hope that offering this reading will point to the simultaneously emerging possibilities and challenges we encounter as we aim to make feminist theory matter and have material consequences.

Coming to new materialism in the situatedness of Swedish feminisms and early childhood

The authors of the present volume celebrate a rich feminist landscape as it enacts the diffractive transversal coming-together of scholarly *and* activist thought *and* research in a creative mixture. The political aspects of feminist scholarship in the study of children, childhoods and education are persistently and skilfully brought to the fore. The ambition of the authors' reading of feminist scholarship *into* each other, rather than as one scholarship differing *from* the other, is not just truly feminist but also an accurate and scholarly important objective in feminist new materialist and post-humanist research. This is done, in particular, in Chapter 4, where Kerry Robinson and Jen Lyttleton-Smith negotiate the intersections and tensions of the inclusion of different theoretical readings of gender in childhood from their personal, political and academic experiences.

Some of us, who were reawakened and given new energy to reinvigorate the important work of Donna Haraway (1988a, 1991), Elizabeth Grosz (1994a), Elizabeth Wilson (2004), Anne Fausto-Sterling (2000), Evelyn Fox Keller (1989) among other transdisciplinary thinkers, by ways of Karen Barad's groundbreaking book *Meeting the Universe Halfway* in 2007, were taken by the possibilities of thinking the agency of matter. However, as Debbie Epstein (p. 53, this volume) comments, in hindsight, this can be seen to have rather become a fashionable turn to the *expense* of gender- and sexuality-politics. Epstein argues that the focus on matter can have the potential 'to trivialize or obscure larger concerns of inequality ... [and] potentially "losing sight of the sedimentary layering of power in society"' (p. 52). The situated reading I want to share with you offers a possibility of understanding why this might have happened through the specific writings and theoretical inputs embedded in what I will describe as a Swedish socio-historical situatedness. This particular socio-historical setting mattered for how I would perform my research and produce writings at the time following the publication of Karen Barad's (2007) book. Epstein's important critical analysis is in line with the self-critique I would later offer in a more recent writing (Lenz Taguchi, 2017). Let me elaborate on all of this below.

Being one of the very first scholars to bring Karen Barad's theorizing to early childhood and educational research it mattered – *in terms of situatedness* – that I wrote my book on an intra-active pedagogy (Lenz Taguchi, 2010) in the context of the transgressive work that had been going on in Swedish early childhood during more than a decade. At this time, gender equality practices in preschools and schools had already become more or less a norm in Sweden.[1] This was, at least, something teachers were well aware of and claimed they were supposed to be doing, whether they liked it or not (Eidevald & Lenz Taguchi, 2011). The state investigation for gender-equality in preschool initiated in 2003 came to be associated with the motto: 'gender equality must start with the youngest'. This investigation, in which I was one of the delegates, pushed the government to issue money to gender studies departments in order for them to educate so-called 'gender-pedagogues' to work in preschools and schools – one for each of the 290 municipalities in Sweden. With later reforms, the aim was changed to one gender-pedagogue per school/preschool unit, which might include up to ten preschools and/or schools. In 1998 the first professor in Gender Studies was appointed at Umeå University, and the discipline would become established, strong and respected during the upcoming decade at all the major universities in Sweden. As Liinason (2011: 31) describes the situation in her inquiry of the construction of gender research in Sweden in terms of a success story: 'an institutionalization of feminist ideas in public policies, state regulations and academic practices has taken place'.

A feminist political party – *Feministiskt initiativ* – was founded in 2005 but has so far never passed the 4 per cent limit to get seats in the parliament. In the latest election it got under 1 per cent of the votes. This might, at least in part, be explained by the fact that the latest government called itself a feminist government, which even claims to enact a feminist foreign policy. As a matter of fact, all sitting prime ministers, whether social democrat, liberal or conservative, had made it their habit of calling themselves feminist since 1996, when Göran Persson entered office and would some years later become the first prime minister to do so. By the time of the publishing of Karen Barad's book, thousands of educators in Swedish preschools had, together with me and my academic colleagues, come a long way in strengthening and creating gender-aware practices and an active gender-pedagogy as integrated practices with ongoing play and learning practices, which were the recommended practices by the National School Agency. In compulsory schooling, a queer-theoretically informed norm-critical pedagogy would become recommended practice and would later become a mandatory and examined content in the curriculum of social studies.

To summarize. In the Swedish cultural context at the time when new materialism became established in child studies and early education in Sweden, the socio-historical situatedness can be understood as, at least *discursively*, dominated by a feminist and gender-equal discourse; that is an awareness among educators of why gender- and norm-critical pedagogy is advocated for and what it is supposed to achieve in terms of making future citizens gender-equal.[2] In this context of gender-equality and feminism as a discursive platform, the agency of matter that Barad (2007) proposed in her book seemed to us both new and exciting, as a part of our ongoing gender- and norm-pedagogical work. Barad's theorizing made it easier to show the intra-active performativity of gendered learning contents, play toys, and the practices of using materialities in playgrounds and preschools (e.g. Lenz Taguchi, 2008, Hultman & Lenz Taguchi, 2011; Palmer, 2011). The way I, and my colleagues, put Barad's (2007) and Deleuze and Guattari's (1987) theories to work in a partly uncritical fashion was – at least in part – produced as an effect of the above-described feminist and gender-equal discourse. Hence, in line with the internal critique offered in the interviews in Chapter 3 with Debbie Epstein, Mindy Blaise, Veronica Pacini-Ketchabaw and Jen Lyttleton-Smith in this volume, I am first in line to endorse this self-critical discussion of this perhaps unfortunate less 'standpointed' and overly materialist way of putting new materialist theory to work. Not the least because this take-up is still prevailing, not only in undergraduate and graduate work but also in the work of more established researchers.

Moreover, for those of us feminist post-structuralists who had read Donna Haraway and Judith Butler in the 1990s in a fashion where the biological body was mutually constitutive of subjectivity, Barad's (2007) and Alaimo and Hekman's (2008) books plugged right into our – since long – frustration about the claim that everything is socially constructed by meaning-making discourse. The dominance of the social construction of gender was something that Alaimo and Susan Hekman (2008) in their preface accused the most dominant feminist voices to desperately cling on to, due to their rightful fear of having the body of women become biologically essentialized. There was, however, no clear *shift* or *turn* to the material, as the authors in this volume all give a voice to in one way or another (see especially Chapters 3 and 4). Rather, they emphasize the importance of acknowledging the interdependencies between multiple feminisms in order to find ways to maintain the connections and relations. This is also one of the main arguments in Nina Lykke's (2010) important book *Feminist Studies* in which she suggests the term '*post*constructionist' feminism to underscore this interdependence. As Osgood and Robinson write in this volume, with reference to Hughes and Lury (2013), we were and should not be blinded by the 'new' in new materialism: rather we need to highlight

> the persistence of long-standing feminist concerns with positionality, relationality and interdisciplinarity, with what can be known and who can be a knower, and with the centrality of ethical, transformative practices within relations of power, as well as the acknowledgement that we live in, and are of, a more-and-other-than-human world. (p. 35, this volume)

In relation to the above, it is important to acknowledge that Haraway's (1988) suggested methodological practices of situated knowledge and situatedness evolved from her interdisciplinary knowing and transdisciplinary engagement *with*, and in the intersections *between*, the sciences of the body and earth, social *and* humanities sciences. Haraway, Fausto-Sterling, Fox-Keller, Grosz and Wilson – among others – had since as early as the 1990s already convincingly argued for the co-constitutiveness of sex and gender. They, in part, drew upon contemporary scientific theories and findings, such as the emerging theories of epigenetics, and the empirical findings of brain-plasticity from the early 1960s, in the research of Marian Diamond (Diamond et al., 1964) as one of the first women neuroscientists. With this in mind, a feminist academic such as myself, who like Barad had an interest in physics, biology, genetics, the neurosciences and medicine, I felt that Barad's theorizing helped me re-engage with all of that earlier feminist work in a way that helped me write better on the co-constitutiveness of discourse and matter. Thus, my own and others' writings on the embodiment of subjectivity, the body, and the embodied brain – the 'brain-body-in-culture' (e.g. Pitts-Taylor, 2016; Schmitz, 2016) – could now evolve as more closely corresponding to our personal experiences of our own bodies and subjectivities (Lenz Taguchi, 2013; Lenz Taguchi & Palmer, 2013).

What I want to argue in relation to the above is that in the wider international community of feminist researchers in child studies and education, we came to new materialism and post-humanism from somewhat different entry points. These were more or less political in kind – in terms of standpoints – due to the situatedness of the socio-classed-raced-sexualized-gendered-cultural contexts from which we wrote our research or did our academic activist work. In my own academic and sociocultural situatedness, feminism, sex- and gender-politics constituted an already established platform. On this platform the turn to materiality appeared in our writings to be more or less *a*political or at least definitely less 'standpointed' as an effect of the context in which they were written.

The situated setting of Swedish teacher education and preschools

To reconnect to Colebrook's quote above: what did my own and my colleagues' work become productive of in the socio-historical situatedness in a large number of preschools mainly around Stockholm? By ways of textbooks for teacher education and in-service training lectures – featuring feminist post-structuralism and feminist new materialism – our academic work has indeed come to matter in the practices of preschool and school practices. The curriculum in the preschool teacher education programme at Stockholm University (3½ years of university training) has been based on sociocultural and social constructionist theories during the last decade (cf. Vallberg-Roth, 2018). In Stockholm and some smaller towns around Sweden, critical and post-structural theories are also a strong feature, including feminist theory, deconstruction, power analysis, positioning analysis, etc., and with entries of new materialist intra-active pedagogy (Lenz Taguchi, 2012), Deleuzian literacy theory (Olsson, 2013). In this specific academic educational setting, the above-named theoretical approaches had thus become the norm while other approaches, such as developmental theories, had become almost completely abandoned. Thus, in contrast to the Australian Anglo-cultural context that Mindy Blaise and Bronwyn Davies describe in their interviews in Chapter 3 of this volume, the only traces left were historical perspectives where 'old' theorists such as Jean Piaget, Eric Homburger Ericson and Arnold Gesell were taught in a straw-man fashion. These developmental theories were taught and viewed in simplified ways and pushed aside, as the 'new' critical feminist and social constructionist approaches became increasingly established as the 'new' and better theories to put to practice.

In this section, I want to put the above-described situated context of preschool teacher education in Stockholm in relation to what is described in some of the texts of the present volume. I specifically want to highlight the references to practices dominated by what seems to be the dominant 'discourses of developmentalism and childhood innocence' (p. 48). This is a discourse which, in the Anglo-cultural early childhood context, is described as in urgent need to be challenged by a feminist post-structural, new materialist and post-humanist discourse. What I want to argue is that these *situated* descriptions of the limitations and risks of a developmental psychological discourse offered in the writings of this volume – valid in an Anglo-cultural context – when read in the Swedish context, merely fuel the already established straw-man image understood as developmental psychology. However, this straw-man image is also supported by the (early) writings by myself (1997/2013), Dahlberg, Moss and Pence (1999/2013) and others, which are still included and read in teacher education all over the country. The effect of this is that students in teacher education think of developmental psychology as a historical phenomenon, which early childhood education still needs to be safeguarded from. In this sense, the straw-man image serves to keep the old 'ghost' of developmentalism safely at bay. This has, however, some specific material consequences that I will now turn to.

Turning to educators in preschool practices, multiple ways of understanding a child's identity/subjectivity construction exist side by side, depending on when and where an educator has been educated (Aronsson & Lenz Taguchi, 2018; Vallberg-Roth, 2018). However, when considering the particular material and discursive setting of Swedish preschools and Swedish preschool education – *again stressing the situatedness* – it would be grossly misleading to describe Swedish preschool teachers in the same terms as that which is offered in the present volume in terms of being 'locked into a moral order (Deleuze), where they don't have to think, where they are in a constant line of descent. The possibility of something new is not there' (p. 50). Arguably, the situatedness of Swedish preschools described above rather begs for an analysis that directs attention to what the powerful discourses and practices of norm-critical and gender-pedagogical approaches have produced. These have opened up for practices of meta- and self-reflection. In preschools, such practices emerged from the early practices of what was called 'deconstructive talks' which were introduced as part of pedagogical documentation practices in the late 1990s (Lenz Taguchi, 2000, 2007, 2008). Through analysing their own analyses of children's creative work and behaviour, these deconstructive talks helped teachers to *reconstruct* their thinking and practices (Åberg & Lenz Taguchi, 2005/2018; Lenz Taguchi, 2008). In this sense, reconstruction as an effect of deconstructive self-reflection has been the core idea in the transformative practices introduced by Gunilla Dahlberg (Dahlberg et al. 1999/2013), myself (Lenz Taguchi, 1997/2013, 2000, 2007, 2008) and others (Olsson, 2009, 2013; Palmer, 2011). This is not to say that de/reconstructing talking about everyday practices has become a self-evident and widespread evaluation strategy. Reflecting on your own practice is, however, a required practice as part of yearly self-evaluations performed by the whole staff (Moberg, 2018). The point is, though, that we need to describe and consider the specific theoretical ideas that are circulated, taken up and transformed in, in this case, Swedish preschools. An additional remark needs to be made at this point. Although there is no influential developmentalist curriculum in the Swedish preschool context, as in the form referred to in the Anglo-cultural context, the straw-man image still gets circulated among teachers and researchers. It is used to make visible to teachers what they are *not supposed to be doing* when describing their own desired practices. This is in line with the tendency in critical and feminist post-structuralist work to point to non-desirable ways of thinking when describing the desirable theory, methodology and practice, as if these can only be described as a difference *from* (e.g. Lenz Taguchi, 1997/2013).

Now to the material consequences of what has been described above. The simplified straw-man images of developmentalism which is still present in the Swedish context and the negative logic when describing your desired practices in terms of difference *from* that image have led to a profound disinterest and rejection of what had been and is currently going on in other academic disciplines that are researching different aspects of children's learning and development. Furthermore, the oversimplification and overuse of the social constructionist theories and practices have made these theories normative in the same way we used to think about 'the old developmentalist' theories (Aronsson & Lenz Taguchi, 2018). The effect of any discourse becoming a new norm constitutes, as we know, a power production that renders all other discourses and connected practices redundant.

The above examples illustrate how significant geopolitical context is. How might we understand the relation between that which is local and situated, and a grander and more powerful discourse at work on a general level? Especially when we might also conclude that what is situated and specific is also dependable and interwoven with that which is considered general. This refers to a very difficult and complex feminist issue, which sometimes causes a conflict that polarizes between practising feminism as in taking a *political standpoint position* on a general level *and* practising a feminism which emphasizes the analysis of the *situated and local.* This issue can also be referred to the problematic relation between a structuralist feminism and the post-structural feminism, which was subject of fierce debates in the 1990s (e.g. Hekman, 1990; Flax, 1993). One way of dealing with this problematic tension is to do a turn to ontology, as is the case with new materialism and post-humanist feminist research as these theories refer to a relational, flat and immanent ontology. Diffraction is often put forward as a possible way of theorizing in a non-polarizing manner as part of such a relational and immanent ontology. With references to Haraway (1988) and Barad (2007), waves of diffraction, as in sound waves or light waves, come to illustrate how former theories and practices are always also a part of the transformations into the 'new'. Osgood and Robinson, in this volume, theorize correspondingly in a very productive manner on 'matters of dis/continuity' and the 'generative' aspects of feminism(s) as they work across/within/through borders (pp. 2–3, this volume). As I move to the last section, I want to affirm and embrace this important way of conceptualizing the conditions for feminist knowledge production and activist work. I also want to offer an additional way of thinking and doing academic work, which can become productive together with doing diffractive movements.

Diffraction processes and individuating self-differentiating in a relation to other self-differentiating bodies and matter

In relation to the argumentation above, it is crucial for me as a feminist to avoid any polarizing between standpoint positionings vs. the situatedness of knowing/knowledge, the general vs. the specific, the body vs. social construction and discourse vs. matter. I want to call for the necessary coexistence and entanglement of diffractive processes *and* the simultaneous individuating processes of self-differentiating of bodies in a relation to other bodies and environments. This is done through combining my readings of Barad's (2007) and Deleuze and Guattari's (1987) philosophies as two partly different ontologies working together. My reading of the following quote by Colebrook constitutes one possible way of summarizing this simultaneous move when read together with an important add-on in brackets:

> Every female is an individuated actualization of a genetic potential for sexual differentiation, and every aspect of that female body – ranging from chromosomal and hormonal composition to the stylization of dress and comportment – is one highly individuated way of actualizing a potentiality [emerging in the relation with other individuated and actualized bodies and the environment in which they coexist]. (Colebrook, 2014: 105)

I work with this quote as a means to theorize how gender, sexuality, subjectivity, etc., express and actualize themselves in relation to two important statements made in the present volume. Bronwyn Davies and Debbie Epstein, respectively, raise two definitive points that no feminist can shy away from. Davies talks about the difficulties of lasting change. Such difficulties are due to our tendency to 'go back into the already known, and because of *the way the new actually depends on, is inter-woven with, the already known*' (p. 55, italics added). Furthermore, Epstein asks: '*How do the privileged remain in place?*' (p. 52). It is possible, the way I read these quotes, to put them side by side with the notion of a feminism that is *simultaneously* constituted by the situated *and* by a more general standpoint position. This is, in fact, how I also understand what Osgood and Robinson (p. 35, this volume) are saying in the earlier quote.

In the above, I have sketched a situated setting of Swedish early childhood as constituted by a social constructionist and feminist norm-critical platform, but by the end of the day, *the privilege of the majoritarian still remains*. Why are women and children still, and in a very decisive way, more often treated as lesser than men, although the discourses and practices do not reveal this? In a recent novel, the Swedish journalist Jenny Nordlander (2018) shows how in journalism women outnumber men, and all practices are and appear gender-equal, but the subtle everyday communication practices of making women feel lesser than men prevail. We recognize all the signs from the world of the (Swedish) academy as well: practices exercised by 'soft' men calling themselves feminist and doing feminist research as their everyday academic practices. Hence, there is a concise way in which men, or the richer and whiter, will always secure their privileges somehow. How does it work? How is this privileging achieved, produced and done?

Going back to Davies's emphasis on our tendency to 'go back into the already known' in the construction of the new, I wish to point to the risks and dangers of the 'already known' – such as notions and old patterns of oppression – reappearing in the disguise of the new. In my reading of Davies, she refers to our tendency to relate all new knowledge phenomena to what we have already learned. What we have already learned always has what can be understood as a primary privileged position in our knowledge constructing mind. It has already created a place for itself and constitutes that which *might* – or might not – be transformed when encountering and being involved with something new. This is why the new sometimes merely is made into a slightly different shape of the old, *while maintaining the force of the former's privilege*. To clarify. This learning does therefore not involve a transformative learning that means that a new knowledge phenomenon is *added* and placed *besides* the first on an equal level: to work *together with it* or to challenge its shape, meaning or articulation. Rather, making the new into a new version of the old also seems to happen when we in a linear and progressive fashion shift our preferences, values or beliefs. This means that we replace one value or theory with another (better) one, without acknowledging and maintaining what might be important to still know or value in the former. This, I argue, blocks the possibilities of putting different ways of knowing or valuing side by side in order to understand what they do differently and how they might individually self-differentiate and transform in themselves (Lenz Taguchi, 2017). Replacing one with the other is how I, in a former piece of writing, without reflecting on the material consequences, made a turn from one ontology (phenomenology) to another (immanence) (Lenz Taguchi, 2013). The material consequence of this is an enactment of the practices of a classical dichotomous worldview, choosing one over the other and disregarding the knowledge production of the former as of lesser value or, alternatively, a reinstatement of the old in new disguise. With profound self-awareness, I need to acknowledge that this is also what we risk doing, as I and my colleagues are currently introducing the new developmental sciences in our early childhood teacher education programme. The force of the (earlier privileged) developmental sciences might re-emerge to diminish the force of the presently privileged social constructionist and sociocultural dominance and weaken it to its former lesser position. The risk of a backlash (Faludi, 1994) is present in what I still consider a necessary move towards the multiple.

How then might it be possible to, without becoming naively relativistic in our *both-and ambitions*, navigate this terrain of a dangerous labyrinth with many detours? Our cause is to acknowledge a reality of *multiple* and *simultaneous* ontologies and epistemologies, working together and sometimes in conflict with each other, which will have them self-differentiate (Lenz Taguchi, 2017) in their encounters. Depending on the matter of concern, one might be given a stronger influence than the other but without having one become privileged in a way that it becomes oppressive of another. In the realm of academic knowledge production around an important shared matter of concern, I grasp for a collaboration across *different* ways of knowing a reality of necessarily multiple realities (ontologies) and ways of knowing (epistemologies) (Lenz Taguchi, 2017). Hence, I suggest for us to find ways to acknowledge *multiple ways of knowing* in a relation *with* each other – together. Starting by negotiating, with stakeholders – whether human or non-human – the shared matter of concern for the research. Then negotiating the possible ways of understanding the consequences of what can be learnt, as the results of *multiple* research findings and their necessarily differing epistemological narratives, and what they produce together. This is the way I imagine a possibility of *more* kinds of feminisms working together, and together with researchers from other disciplines. Foremost, I imagine working together with the stakeholders for whom the matter of concern matters the most, whether it is children, women, racialized people, animals or matter in the environment on which we depend for our existence. To make this argument more concrete, let us talk about the shared concern of educating the youngest in the problematics of environmental issues and sustainable living

Revisiting the quote above, I want to argue that with such an important matter of concern, we would definitely need to consult many different disciplines of knowledge production. Elkin Postila (submitted) is pursuing research in collaboration with forty-seven preschool children investigating environmental issues concerning water and the rising water levels. She engages knowledge from the fields of the geosciences, engineering, botany, ecology, biology and early childhood education. We need to explore what knowledge from these various academic disciplines might achieve when put in relation to each other with their respective and multiple ways of knowing the matter of concern: while still honouring their respective differences, something similar is undertaken by Osgood via an experiment with Lego, in Chapter 5 of this volume. In diffractive engagements with each other, the different collaborating epistemologies thus *maintain* their own basic *but porous* disciplinary shapes, while honouring these porous borders between each other in a process of simultaneous mutual and individuating self-differentiating transformation (cf. Lenz Taguchi, 2017; Aronsson, submitted). This also refers to the potential equality between them, while highlighting the various layers of ethics in the process of simultaneously contributing with knowledge production and collaborating with each other. In my experience, this can only be done while honouring the ethical engagement with this particular and situated matter of concern, in terms of all the various agents and actors involved (Frankenberg et al., 2018).

Last but not least. In relation to this volume, where some of the field's finest feminist scholars appear, who persistently engage in 'the acknowledgement that we live in, *and* are of, a more-and-other-than-human world', I want to acknowledge that there are, in fact, many researchers in other disciplines that do the same, while relying on differing and other ontologies and epistemologies in their respective knowledge production. Let us, as positioned but simultaneously situated and self-differentiating feminists, reach out to them and make a difference!

Notes

1 Preschool in Sweden is a full-day provision constituting the first step of the Swedish educational system, enrolling 84 per cent of the one- to three-year-old children and 96 per cent of the four- and five-year-olds with working or studying guardians. It is a subsidized system that costs the government app. 1.3 per cent of GDP yearly, with a maximum fee of 3 per cent of the household income for the first child. There are lower fees for each additional child and there is no fee for child number four and onwards. By the autumn term when the child will turn three years old, the municipality must offer the child at least 525 hours each year. Also children with parents who are not working must be offered at least 15 hours/ week. On average there are 15.9 children per group and a ratio of 5.2 children to one adult across all ages, but the variations are large between municipalities and services (for more information visit Swedish National Agency for Education, https://www.skolverket.se)

2 https://www.skolverket.se/skolutveckling/forskning-och-utvarderingar/forskning/ makt-normer-och-delaktighet-en-utmaning-for-forskolan.

Acknowledgements

The creation of this book gestated over several years and was born of myriad feminist entanglements encompassing friendships (old, new and virtual), geographical continents, the passage of years, chance and planned encounters, micro events, digital teleconferencing technologies, conference papers and symposia, breakfast meetings, protest marches, online/offline connectivity, email, companion cats, wine and laughter. But it has been a seriously playful and playfully serious business. We felt we *needed* to write this book; we were confronted in equal measure by unease, as we were enthusiasm, for the possibilities presented by the 'new materialist turn' in feminist research. It was the 'newness' that troubled us most. We wondered: what was especially 'new' about this approach; and did taking up the 'new' mean discarding the 'old'? It seemed to us that the ways in which we had approached the study of childhood and gender for sometime were under threat! Were we done with that which we were so familiar? That which had served us so well. That which we believed continued to hold the capacity to do important feminist work: to trouble and unsettle taken-for-granted 'truths' about gendered childhoods; to deconstruct obvious and seemingly reasonable accounts of gendered childhoods. Could the 'new' still allow us to insist that gender matters in early childhood? What affordances might feminist 'new' materialism make possible? How might it work in productive partnership with feminist post-structuralist approaches? How could bringing materiality and affect more forcibly into the frame of our investigations insist upon the continuing, and renewed, importance of gender in childhood? These questions provided the driving force for this project.

We owe a debt of gratitude to the wealth of feminist scholars who are cited throughout this book; their insights and ideas, philosophies and activisms have inspired and nourished us. We especially want to extend our thanks to Bronwyn Davies, Debbie Epstein, Mindy Blaise, Veronica Pacini-Ketchabaw and Jen Lyttleton-Smith for coming on this feminist adventure with us. The value of their wisdom, scepticism, passion, politics and creativity was enormous to the realization of this project. It was their willingness to enter into difficult conversations about where feminist thought in childhood studies has been, and is going, that provides the backbone to this volume. Bringing generations of feminist scholars into conversation with each other was always going to be a lively, messy and generative affair but what these conversations produced underlines the importance of re-turning and staying with the trouble, insisting on being troublemakers and questioning, deeply, how feminist politics can remain in play when 'new' theories and methodologies are mobilized.

This book was a collaborative experiment that was only possible because of interwoven, multilayered, dynamic processes of feminist praxis. We endeavoured to push against the normative model of what an edited book should be. Our goal was that it would be a transversal exercise concerned as much with the processes involved in its creation as the end product. We wanted this to be an authentically feminist project that was respectful of diverse feminist approaches to childhood studies and that lay bare the processes of feminist knowledge production. Such ambitions made untold demands on us, and without the support and openness of our publishers at Bloomsbury Academic, it would not have been possible. Mark Richardson and Maria Brauzzi were willing to embrace our non-normative ways of presenting ideas and practices in this edited volume and for that we thank them. We also thank them for their patience and compassion when, at times, ill health and other unforeseen demands knocked us off schedule.

We also thank our peers, colleagues and students who have engaged with some of the ideas in this book as we have presented and debated them at various seminars, conferences and in-between spaces over the past few years. The questions and comments we have encountered have pushed us to grapple deeply with our emergent arguments and ideas. We would like to pay special mention to the Childhood & Society SIG at Middlesex University; the International PhEMaterialism Network; Nordic colleagues within the Performing Methodologies in Early Years Education Research (PMEYER); Social Justice in Early Childhood (SJIEC, Australia); the Gender and Education Association (specifically its Conference in 2017); colleagues at ESRI, Manchester Metropolitan University; colleagues in Sexualities and Genders Research (SaGR) and those in the School of Social Sciences and Psychology, and the Centre for Education Research, at Western Sydney University; our co-editors at the journals: *Gender and Education, Reconceptualising Educational Research Methodology* and *Contemporary Issues in Early Childhood*. These networks, events and connections are complex and generative. In early childhood the adage that it takes a village to raise a child reminds us that it takes worldly entanglements with countless others (human, non-human and more-than-human) to raise a book from the kernel of an idea to fruition. We thank you all.

Life as feminist academics in the post-Anthropocene presents certain challenges. Writing projects, such as this book, come replete with demands made of, within and by neo-liberal universities. This book has been a 'performance indicator'; it has demanded strategies to maximize 'impact' – that we reach our 'market' and that it is guaranteed to have a demonstrable positive effect on student engagement, satisfaction and attainment. As neo-liberal subjects we must make our labour and outputs transparent, measurable, quantifiable, REF-able, TEF-able, ultimately knowable and scrutinizable. Located as we are within this milieu, we draw on our feminist sensibilities to find ways to resist, subvert and reconfigure. Like many other feminist scholars we live life on the margins, in the liminal spaces, where we can create ruptures and persistently question that which is inequitable and unjust. We appreciate the space that our respective institutions, Middlesex University and the Western Sydney University, have given us and their belief that the projects we toil over are important and worth supporting.

Finally, in dedicating this book we want to dwell on the well-established feminist phrase 'the personal is political'. For us, as daughter, mother, sister, aunt, the personal struggles, juggles and joys that we encounter in our routine everyday lives provide us with the inspiration and motivation to agitate, activate and insist upon a feminist reading of, and becoming with, the world. The smallest cuts matter. We find ourselves in the extraordinarily privileged position of creating opportunities to theorize, research and debate issues of gendered childhoods. We do this because it matters; for us it is a feminist matter of concern. We dedicate this book to our respective menageries, and all the human, non-human and other-than-human inhabitants.

1

Introduction: Throwing the Baby out with the Bathwater? Traces and Generative Connections between Feminist Post-structuralism and Feminist New Materialism in Childhood Studies

Jayne Osgood and Kerry H. Robinson

> But in any case, creativity is not about crafting the new through a radical break with the past. It's a matter of dis/continuity, neither continuous nor discontinuous in the usual sense. It seems to me that it's important to have some kind of way of thinking about change that doesn't presume there's more of the same or a radical break. Dis/continuity is a cutting together-apart (one move) that doesn't deny creativity or innovation but understands its indebtedness and entanglements to the past and the future. (Barad, cited in Juelskjaer & Schwennesen, 2012: 16)

A matter of dis/continuity

In the spirit of Barad's insistence of the indebtedness and entanglements to past and future, this collaborative feminist book project sets out to explore the ways in which feminist researchers have approached the study of children, childhood, gender and sexualities over the past thirty years or so. There is a growing body of feminist scholarship that takes up new materialist approaches, and our concern is to trace how this departs from, and is continuous with, the important post-structuralist work that so profoundly shifted debates, practices and policies around gender and sexualities in childhood.

Since the late 1980s and 1990s, post-structuralist philosophies and practices shaped approaches to childhood research in significant ways. Much of the research at that time owed a debt to the theorizations of gender offered by Judith Butler. Most notable was her conceptualization of gender as performative which highlights the significance of everyday routines, performances and interactions that shape gendered behaviours and contribute to the formation of gendered identities. Her insistence that gender is socially constructed as opposed to biologically determined or learnt; that gender is fluid and shifting and hinges upon the context in which it is performed was transformative to how gender in childhood is researched. While Butler's work continues to shape the field of childhood studies, there has been a recent emergence of a growing body of new materialist and post-humanist approaches which invites a re-examination of how we come to understand children and childhood – which also foregrounds context, fluidity and performance but which brings materiality and affect more forcibly into the frame. While research within these traditions takes many forms, our concern is to trace how *feminist* researchers work with the philosophies on offer to approach the study of gender and sexuality as it plays out in childhood.

This book aims to foreground the F-word within these shifting, mutating and growing theoretical and methodological currents. We are concerned with *feminist* post-structuralist and *feminist* new materialist research and with unearthing what working within these frameworks can afford feminist researchers in their pursuit of knowledge production for more liveable worlds (Haraway, 2015) where children are working through ideas and embodied encounters with gender and sexuality. Feminist scholarship is concerned with everyday life and ordinary experiences and is underpinned by political motivations to transform inequalities and injustices through critique and reconfiguration. This feminist thread courses through all the work of each contributor to this book.

Generative feminism(s): Working across/within/ through borders

For decades, feminist research has made a crucially important contribution to developing diverse and collaborative ways to understand gender, feminism(s), sexual identities, education and embodied experiences. Attending to social inequities through an intersectional lens, feminist research has exposed how power operates in childhood contexts, taking the personal as political into the heart of research investigations to radically shift how children are conceptualized. By focusing on the role of language in the constitution of social reality, and by demonstrating that discursive practices constitute the social position of women and girls, post-structuralist feminists engaged in important deconstructive work to identify the concepts that define and denigrate. Linguistic and discursive projects of deconstruction have been productive to aid complex analyses of the interconnection between knowledge, power, subjectivity and language (Alaimo & Hekman, 2008). Crucially, feminist post-structuralist scholarship opened up critical ways to understand how gender intersects with social class, race, sexuality and so on to position women and girls within cultural systems of difference that cast them as subordinate, inferior or in some sense other. However, while many social constructionist theories grant the existence of material reality, it is often viewed separately to language, discourse and culture. This presumed separateness has meant that the textual, linguistic and discursive have remained the focus of research, and materiality, the body and nature are viewed as products of discourse. The material turn in feminist research moves away from this privileging of textual representation, systems of thought and discourses and instead emphasizes social production rather than social construction. Or as Haraway states, we must engage in practices of materialized refiguration (1994: 61–62):

> Textual re-reading is never enough, even if one defines the text as the world. Reading however active, is not a powerful enough trope … the trick is to make metaphor and materiality implode in culturally specific apparatuses of bodily production … engaging in the always messy projects of description, narration, invention, inhabiting, conversing, exchanging and building. The point is to get at how worlds are made and unmade, in order to participate in the processes … The point is not just to read the webs of knowledge production; the point is to reconfigure what counts as knowledge in the interests of reconstituting the generative forces of embodiment.

Emergence of the 'new'

The new materialist/affective turn in feminist research has produced a wider range of methodologies and interdisciplinary approaches with which to theorize and research gender. However, the 'newness' of these exciting developments owes an enormous debt to generations of feminist scholars; the aim of this book is to recognize and celebrate the rich feminist landscape. Fox and Alldred (2017: 2) note the lineage from which new materialism emerged:

New materialism has been informed by post-structuralist, feminist, post-colonialist and queer theories, which rejected structuralist determinism as inadequate to critique patriarchy … or to supply a critical and radical stance to underpin struggles for social justice and plurality.

Furthermore, the 'newness' must be treated with caution and placed in context. Questions guiding the creation of this book have included 'what is especially *new* about new materialism?' and 'what is especially *feminist* about feminist new materialism?' While feminist new materialism presents innovative approaches to conceptualizing and grappling with gender issues in education, concerns such as inequalities, violence and power asymmetries have always been foundational to feminist research. We also need to caution against colonizing or appropriating or ignoring indigenous cosmologies such as traditional Maori, Inuit and Aboriginal thought that has for millennia considered the human–natural world as inextricably interwoven so that objects, places, weather patterns, seasons and so on are respected, acknowledged and encountered as material-discursive-semiotic manifestations. Engaging ethically with such worldviews can assist feminist new materialists in working from the premise that we are inseparable from the materiality of the world and our knowledge of it (Coole & Frost, 2010). As Taylor and Ivinson (2013: 666) stress:

By properly recognising that we have no birds-eye position from which to look back or down at our world, we have to take seriously our own messy, implicated, connected, embodied involvement in knowledge production.

Coole and Frost (2010) discuss three interrelated but distinctive directions in new materialist scholarship – first, an ontological reorientation that conceives of matter itself as lively or exhibiting agency; second, a consideration of biopolitical and bioethical issues concerning the status of life and the human; and third, a fresh exploration of the material details of everyday life and broader geopolitical and socio-economic structures. Across these three approaches is a shared emphasis on materialization as a complex, pluralistic and open process where humans (including the researcher) are recognized as thoroughly immersed within materialities. New materialism concerns itself with forces, energies, intensities, affect and complex (sometimes random) processes. New materialist ontologies demand a rethinking of, and renewed attention to, how matter comes to matter. This requires a radical reappraisal of what is meant by subjectivity, a reassessment of ethics and re-examination of power. Decentring the human subject opens possibilities to bring into play unfamiliar frames for reimagining justice and for exploring the wider sources, qualities and dimensions of agency.

Our biggest concern in this book is to attend to the generative, generating and generational potential available in tracing lines through feminist research (Van der tuin, 2015). One important line in feminist thought is that it is our being in the world that grants us knowledge.

> Knowing, thinking, measuring and theorizing, and observing are material practices of intra-acting within and part of the world ... We do not uncover pre-existing facts about independently existing things as they exist frozen in time like little statues positioned in the world. Rather, we learn about phenomena – about specific material configurations of the world's becoming ... the point is not merely that knowledge practices have material consequences but that practices of knowing are specific material engagements that participate in (re) configuring the world. (Barad, 2007: 91)

Feminist post-structuralists (e.g. Butler, 1990; Grosz, 1994) and feminist new materialists (e.g. Barad, 2007; Braidotti, 2013; Haraway, 2008, 2016) foreground ethics and our ethical responsibility to displace any claims to objectivity and detachment from that which we research. Seeking out these dis/continuities across time and space allows us to further contemplate what feminist research is possible of and what it does best: unsettle, intervene and insist upon demonstrable impacts for greater gender equity in educational policy, practical pedagogies and within communities. The politically motivated practices of feminist researchers are present across post-structuralist and new materialist studies; the persistence of gender as an issue and a problem in childhood contexts acts to continuously drive our investigations, experimentations and our insistence that gender in childhood must be understood differently in ways that are more ethical and recognize the shifting and specific contexts in which childhoods play out. This outrage can generate guides to action that take account of complexity:

> Outrage will not and should not disappear, but a politics devoted too exclusively to moral condemnation and not enough to cultivated discernment of the web of agentic capacities can do little good ... An understanding of agency as confederate thus involves the need to detach ethics from moralism and to produce guides to action appropriate to a world of vital, cross-cutting forces. (Bennett, 2010: 38)

Feminist researchers are outraged; it is outrage that motivates and drives our research – a desire to address injustice, prejudice, oppression. Ahmed's (2017) figure of the 'feminist killjoy' finds expression in how we endeavour to live our lives and make a difference in the world. Naming discourses, critiquing policies and practices, and problematizing and unsettling taken-for-granted 'truths' are all vital tools for the feminist researcher. Furthermore, the work of Braidotti, Haraway and Barad among others presents the feminist researcher with possibilities to reconfigure what we think we see and what we think we know (about gender and sexualities in childhood). Working with the material and the affective in childhood studies generates new knowledges and new ways of viewing and being in the world.

Enacting feminist politics in research

Taking up feminist new materialism involves rupturing our previous efforts to represent and capture gendered lives as they are lived in early childhood contexts and to make space for, acknowledge, and play with that which is routinely written out and invisibilized in conventional research practices. It requires that we take seriously the seemingly unremarkable, insignificant, routine everyday matter, events and becomings within which children are entangled. The shape that research studies take and methods that are employed become reconfigured.

While much post-structuralist feminist research in childhood employs ethnographic methods – and so the material and affective are omnipresent – the emphasis nevertheless tends towards a focus on the human subject by observing, gathering data, capturing accounts and reproducing them in textual form (as observation notes, interview transcripts) that are then subjected to textual analysis to identify discourses and discursive constructions of gendered patterns and problems in early childhood. This scholarship significantly interrupts taken-for-granted truths about children, childhood innocence, developmentalism and heteronormativity and insists that children must be viewed more respectfully as agentic knowing subjects capable of navigating and generating alternative discourses. Despite this important work though, the field of early childhood in its broadest sense persistently falls back into developmentalist logic, and so the task for the feminist researcher is to consistently restate arguments that present gender as more complex, slippery, contingent than normative frameworks allow for.

The current work of feminist new materialist researchers in childhood studies (e.g. Huuki & Renold, 2015; Jones, 2013; Lyttleton-Smith, 2017) seeks to keep in play the need to re-conceptualize the child and childhood, but rather than deconstructing how children are positioned within discourse, the goal is to attend to generating different knowledges about childhood that are situated and where the researcher is active in processes of production. Foregrounding affect and materiality in the research process demands different, more embodied and intra-active methods. Methods and data take on a different form in feminist new materialist studies; they insist that the researcher is immersed, engaged and actively participating in practices that generate other ways to sense and be in the world. What counts as 'method' and what constitutes 'data' are called into question (Lather and St Pierre , 2013). The everydayness of lives lived and attention to microscopic events that unfold in un/predictable ways insist that researchers take up a more vulnerable approach (as non-expert) and embrace capacities to exercise curiosity and wonder (MacLure, 2013).

This is enacted in contemporary studies undertaken by feminist scholars, including Lenz Taguchi (2010), Taylor et al. (2012), Kind (2013), Nxumalo (2016), Gannon (2017), Lloro-Bidart (2017) and Hickey-Moody (2017), among many others. These studies attend to the significance of place, context, histories and inter-species relations through mobile and digital methodologies (e.g. video, sound, photography) and through movement methodologies (e.g. walking, dancing, crafting, performing as method). These 'doing' methodologies clearly mark a shift from the ethnographic practices of the feminist post-structuralist researcher which are more readily recognizable as conventional research methods that fit within a more recognizable study design with discrete and knowable stages. Working across disciplinary boundaries and embracing unconventional embodied and material practices work to produce a different sort of research process. Within this mode of enquiry (recognized as 'post-qualitative', see Koro-Lungberg et al., 2017), the emphasis is placed on the processes and effects of the research as it takes shape rather than a concern with a set of conclusive outputs. Manning (2016) claims that this mode of enquiry requires a reorientation in order that we can enact and be open to the concept of 'research-creation as a mode of activity that is at its most interesting when it is constitutive of new processes. This can only happen if its potential is tapped in advance of its alignments with existing disciplinary methods and institutional structures', and she goes on to stress that 'new processes will likely create new forms of knowledge that may have no means of evaluation within current disciplinary models' (p. 28).

As post-qualitative inquiry, feminist new materialism and arts-based methods are gaining ground in early childhood research; they can appear daunting precisely because the intention is to break free from the constraints (or comforts) of recognizable research approaches and disciplinary models. These 'new' approaches force questions about what counts as valid knowledge production (Lather, 1993). Returning briefly to Manning (2016), she claims that what emerges is 'a call for speculative pragmatism, speculative in the sense that the process remains open to the more-than, and pragmatic in the sense that it is completely invested in its 'something doing" (p. 33). It is evident that this mode of enquiry is deeply political when the feminist agenda remains in place and that it demands that feminist researchers get 'their hands dirty' in the thick of research processes – in the 'something doings'. For early childhood researchers, this is not a radical departure from the form that many ethnographic studies in early childhood contexts take, where it is nearly impossible not to become entangled in the ebb and flow of daily life, routines and messy unpredictable happenings that are bodily, affective and material. But working from a feminist new materialist framework requires that we immerse ourselves more fully in the intensities, flows, rhythms, affects and forces of children's entanglements with space, place and materiality.

Central to much early childhood research taking up the methodological and onto-epistemological challenges of working within a feminist new materialist framework is the SF philosophy put forward by Donna Haraway through her corpus of work spanning over thirty years but culminating in her most recent book *Staying with the Trouble* (2016) in which she stresses a need to engage in worldling practices. Worldling involves (de)contextualizing the familiar and learning to think in otherworldly ways which involve dis/continuities and tracing through the archives of feminist scholarship to ask the 'what-if' questions and then actively engage in world-making which involves 'deep hanging out' (Haraway, 2016).

Deep hanging out for feminist new materialist researchers researching with children insists upon a different starting point; rather than gathering data to answer a predefined set of questions, the goal is more open-ended and uncertain; the ultimate aim is to produce new knowledges, new ways of sensing and being in the world; and it is within processes of creative experimentation, exercising curiosity and resisting habitual ways of seeking out what is already known, that gender (as processes of becoming in micro-moments) can be reimagined. These examples also demonstrate how these researchers, through 'doing' methodologies, keep in place the political motivations underpinning their work to pursue issues of gender, class, race and disability. This is important to underscore since one of the greatest concerns for sceptics and those new to feminist new materialism is that post-humanist approaches erase humanist concerns. However, the philosophies offered by Ahmed, Barad, Braidotti and Haraway, alongside these post-qualitative examples, demonstrate that, in fact, there is heightened awareness and attention to these issues in feminist new materialist modes of enquiry. New feminist materialism invites an engagement with the (extra)ordinary that is to be found in the routine everyday events in early childhood, the everyday that can be explored through an engagement with processes of becoming that recognizes the productive capacity of the minor gesture (Manning, 2016) to provide the means to view children and their entangled place more generatively. This is what Ahmed (2006) conceptualizes as orientations:

> The starting point for orientation is the point from which the world unfolds: the 'here' of the body and the 'where' of its dwelling. Orientations, then are about the intimacy of bodies and their dwelling places ... Bodies may become orientated in this responsiveness to the world around them ... In turn, given the histories of such responses, which accumulate as impressions of the skin, bodies do not dwell in spaces that are exterior but rather are shaped by their dwellings and take shape by dwelling.

Navigating ways through this book

Our hope is that this book might be engaged with diffractively; we invite readers to delve in and read chapters through each other or in isolation, in sequence or more haphazardly. The project we have set ourselves is transversal, not a linear chronology of where we once were as feminist researchers to where we are now. The aim is to illuminate the threads, connections, sticky knots and productive possibilities that come about from a project of this nature. We present our messy collaboration as a means to provoke thought and inspire research practices in early childhood that benefit from layering and weaving feminist research philosophies, methods and practices through each other so that gender in early childhood continues to be a matter of concern with which feminist scholars persist in grappling with so as to extend and generate new and different knowledges and practices.

Following this introductory chapter, the next chapter charts some key feminist philosophies, theories and research studies that have come to shape understandings of childhood and gender in significant ways over the past three decades. We select important events and moments over time to illuminate the means by which feminist thought is interwoven and entangled and re-turns through processes of dis/continuity. Feminist research has profoundly altered the ways in which childhood and children are conceptualized; the significant ways in which gender and sexuality find expression in public debate in contemporary contexts are a direct result of the important feminist scholarship that has persisted over many decades. Reviewing ruptures created by feminist activists, researchers and academics, we identify how these materialized, affective enactments of feminist politics leave traces and, in many senses, shape what is currently being undertaken in the field of childhood studies by feminist researchers today. The chapter acknowledges the important contributions that feminist philosophers and scholars have made to the field and goes on to explore the possibilities that are opened for feminist new materialists to work with ideas about gender and childhood generatively but in ways that recognize their indebtedness to the past. The fundamental purpose of the chapter is to foreground the F-word and to identify the centrality of feminism and feminist thought to the field of early childhood studies and the continued relevance of gender to our investigations. This entails an engagement with the affordances that feminist theory has created to conceptualize the child and childhood in ways that challenge conservative and regressive ideas, policies and practices. Furthermore, the chapter considers how feminist scholars of childhood have taken up post-structuralist and queer theory to further extend understandings of gender and sexuality. The significance of this work to generating more equitable and transformative pedagogies in early childhood education is also considered. This chapter attends to waves; waves of feminist activism, waves of feminist scholarship and waves of feminist research in early childhood education. Waves that reveal generative and generational traces of understandings about gender and sexualities. Attending to the movement of these waves, and specifically to overlaps, exposes the generative possibilities that can be realized through feminist approaches to childhood research. Through charting the waves, we discern the important contribution that feminist research has made to exposing, exploring and experimenting with ideas about gender in early childhood and go on to underline the significance of these contributions to the field and the vital political role that they play in refusing to allow gender to fall off the agenda.

We challenge the notion that there must be some definitive cut with the past and instead argue for the importance of traces and entanglements. Our aim is to offer a re-turning – which involves an openness to re-engage and re-immerse ourselves in the multiple projects of knowledge production that feminist scholars offer to the field. What this vast body of scholarship demonstrates is that gender remains a crucial aspect of all childhoods. Through convictions to problematize, critique, unsettle, map and reconfigure gender in early childhood, a long history of challenging what counts as valid knowledge (Lather, 1993) emerges. We urge that the field continues to interrogate who gets heard and what gets silenced or obscured from view in debates about gender and to consider deeply what queering dominant ideas about gender in early childhood research, theory and practice might make possible.

The generation of this book involved the inclusion of many feminist philosophers as outlined in the preceding chapter, from de Beavouir, to Butler, to Barad via Mohanty, hooks, and Lorde (among many, many others). Chapter 3 reports on discursive accounts that were generated within a collaborative group of seven feminist scholars, variously engaged in debates about the perceived threats and affordances of an apparent 'paradigm shift' (from feminist post-structuralism to feminist new materialism). The discussion offered in this chapter is based upon qualitative interviews conducted by the authors (i.e. Osgood interviewed Veronica Pacini-Ketchabaw, Debbie Epstein and Jen Lyttleton-Smith; meanwhile Kerry Robinson interviewed Mindy Blaise and Bronwyn Davies). Collectively, the group represented a gathering of prominent feminist scholars, at various stages of their academic careers, all undertaking gender research in the field of early childhood, each having made considerable contributions to theorizations of gender in the field. The work of each feminist scholar interviewee has impacted upon our research into gender and sexuality in various ways, to varying degrees, at various times. The interviews were undertaken because they represented a knowable, familiar, tried and tested means to generate 'data', which we could then go on to analyse and to identify a series of discourses that could tell us something about how these feminist scholars perceived and understood the relationship between feminist post-structuralism and feminist new materialism. The interviews provided the feminist scholars with the opportunity to 'voice' concerns about the paradigm 'shift', as well as reflect on the theoretical re-turns and dis/continuities experienced throughout their academic careers and what underpinned shifts (or resistance to shifts) in the approaches taken in research with young children. The aim of the exercise was to identify the strengths, connections, symmetries and tensions between feminist post-structuralism and feminist new materialism.

The interview data provided interesting insights into the theoretical shifts encountered by the feminist scholars, but of particular significance were the perspectives shared on the relationship between feminist post-structuralism and feminist new materialism. The ontological, new materialist or affective turn (as it was variously referred to) was not considered a radical break away from feminist post-structuralism; indeed the relationship was generally viewed as mutually beneficial, building upon and extending the critical perspectives that each brings to epistemological and ontological understandings of the world and to relationships between human, non-human and more-than-human, that is how they are constituted, situated, reconfigured, overlap and are entangled with each other across time, space, geolocation and political contexts. As linguistic, discursive accounts of life, the interview transcripts provided a valuable means through which to examine engagements and identifications with discourse, taken-for-granted knowledge or 'truths' constituted within the discourses, the identification of counter discourses, and the possible impact of discourse upon individual practices.

The next three chapters offer illustrative examples of the affordances of working with multiple feminist perspectives in research committed to exploring gender in childhood that attend to the material-discursive production of knowledge. Chapter 4 is co-authored by Jen Lyttleton-Smith and Kerry Robinson. The co-authorship was a product of the wider collaborative book project – both Jen and Kerry were tangentially entangled (via Jayne, PhD examiner and co-author, and via engagements with each other's written outputs). Jen's onto-epistemological travelling through her PhD research (from Butler to Barad) was particularly pertinent to a project concerned to investigate the generative potential of shifting from feminist post-structuralism to feminist new materialism. Marrying Jen's nomadic doctoral adventures with Kerry's initial scepticism (of what more new materialism can offer to studies of gender in childhood) and her deep engagement with Butlerian philosophy promised to make for an interesting and insightful chapter. However, given that the authors had no prior connection (other than reading each other's work), further compounded by their location in different global time zones and that they had never written together previously, provided the ingredients for a challenging, uncertain, but productive chapter. Within the chapter, different theoretical approaches to analysing and interpreting the ways in which young children's bodies are dressed up in gendering and queering ways are applied. The advantages, intersections, difficulties and tensions associated with different feminist theoretical frameworks are explored. The authors position themselves theoretically and search for critical moments of coalescence within their respective research studies. Sharing a commitment to feminist post-structuralism and queer theory provided fertile ground from which to generate multilayered arguments that bring together, and distinguish, the dis/continuities of feminist post-structuralism and new materialism. The authors unearth the productive potential of layering approaches to theoretically analyse gender in childhood and so reach deepened understandings of how subjects become gendered and how gender, power and inequality intersect and remain shared matters of concern. They argue that post-humanism is most effectively put to work as an additional layer of analysis that enhances rather than replaces an analysis of power and discourse.

The authors explore a reciprocal relationship between their research interpretations of gender performativity and children's clothing and respective understandings of theoretical performativity as feminist scholars of gender and childhood. They stress that transgressive dress-up creates opportunities for the child body to encounter new and, sometimes, queer or otherwise non-normative ways of experiencing gender and sexuality. Through a series of brief data extracts, 'dress' and 'dress-up' are understood as transformative expressions of gender, political and theoretical subjectivity. Through exploring children's negotiation of different gendered subject positions through dress, children's transgressions from gender norms in this process, children's readings of embodied gender, and the ways in which gender norms are regulated in childhood by children and educators, the dualistic discursive distinction between gendered 'dressing' and 'dressing-up' obscures a simultaneous multiplicity of gender subjectivity where these socially weighted terms flatten to produce the self and the other as one and the same.

They conclude by arguing that post-humanism does not constitute a 'paradigm shift' which threatens to render feminist post-structuralism outdated or irrelevant. Methods of layering theoretical approaches invite questions to ask of data that might not otherwise be considered. It is through sedimented expertise and refinement of repeated application by disparate colleagues of varied interest, space and time that the unthought, unnoticed unexplored might be encountered. They contest that feminist post-structuralism remains vital if we are to explore the newer, winding, branching path of feminist new materialism as it weaves around and through it to produce richer ways of investigating gender in childhood.

Next, Jayne Osgood stays with the trouble presented by a material object that is routinely and habitually found in childhood contexts to reconfigure ideas about gender. She takes the humble Lego brick as a starting point to insist that there is an urgent need to take matter seriously so that both recognizable and unanticipated accounts about gender can be explored and extended. Working with Haraway's (2016) SF philosophy, notably her method of string figuring and her concern to tell stories via methods of speculative fabulation, this chapter endeavours to tell different and multiple stories about Lego by re-turning to a range of disciplinary fields and theoretical orientations. Feminist post-structuralist accounts of block play are revisited to consider how gender is understood, assessed and produced in early childhood contexts; layered upon these insights are those generated from a less certain material-discursive otherworldly investigation. A series of guiding questions are attended to: how have childhood materials been theorized over time through different feminist theoretical lenses? And therefore, what claims have been made? What policy, curricular, pedagogical advances, regressions and stagnations have occurred? What do new materialist feminist approaches to the study of gender in childhood, which take matter as a starting point, offer to existing debates? The chapter concludes by arguing that gender can be reconfigured when Lego is taken as something to think with. Lego can be thought about as imbued with thing-power, carrying and transmitting traces of other assemblages within and stemming from a Lego assemblage that opens up ideas about how gender is more than an exclusively human(ist) matter of concern. The chapter recognizes that the ways in which gender is produced in early childhood are complex and made up of physical flows, languages, gendered discourses, visceral feelings and cultural practices. However, taking the liveliness of matter; asking what Lego does, and what we might do with what it does, offers a multilayered, speculative account that opens up endless possibilities. 'Rummaging around looking for the parts' allowed for the generation of other stories about gender – stories comprised of entangled knots, patterns, string figures; troubling and hopeful stories; speculative fabulation. Through processes of scavenging, foraging and wayfaring, the generation of this chapter involved tentacular processes of sensing, feeling, making connections of possibility to connect complex stories that relate to each other (Haraway, 2016: 2) and that intend to offer other ways in which to encounter ideas and practices in early childhood contexts.

The third illustrative example of the generative potential of dis/continuous feminist epistemologies is offered by Mindy Blaise and Veronica Pacini-Ketchabaw through an examination of movement pedagogies in early childhood and how they produce gender (differently). They return to the highly problematic hegemony of developmental and binary logic shaping early childhood education. As feminist scholars working in early childhood education, they are troubled by binarized thinking about gender for how it reinforces gender norms and gender stereotypes, while also constructing a gender-neutral child. The authors seek to establish how feminist materialist movement pedagogies are part of a gender politics that hold the potential to unsettle foundational and developmental thinking. The chapter outlines three shifts within theory (developmental, feminist post-structuralist, feminist new materialist) that change pedagogies by attending to gender differently. Data from a movement inquiry in Canada illuminates how feminist new materialist theories might be enacted in practice.

The movement inquiry was intended to reconfigure how moving bodies are thought about. As such, these feminist movement pedagogies do more than just reconfigure bodies; they also *activate new political thought*. This is a shift away from simply being concerned with supporting a child's linear growth and development, towards rethinking movement itself.

The authors investigate how feminist movement pedagogies produce child gendered bodies – recognizing them as transversal, occurring in moments where entanglements are sensed corporeally – and therefore challenge normative understandings of motor development as unfolding in a linear direction. Feminist materialist movement pedagogies insist upon other modes of enquiry – ones that question how gendered and more-than-human bodies are activated and what they produce. Feminist materialist movement pedagogies are uncertain and unscripted, requiring a logic of unknowability, a logic of openness and a logic of uncertainty which challenges both developmental and feminist post-structuralist logic. To convey what might be involved in such a speculative pedagogy, the authors therefore present a short photo essay as provocation about how emergence and unknowability might be activated in early childhood education. Each photo highlights the inventive political potential of feminist materialist movement pedagogies to destratify gender binaries. The reorganization of bodies through human and non-human movements does not erase gender but acts to multiply gender beyond binary divisions, to traverse gender-dominant alignments and to create new connections that disrupt what is anticipated, stepping outside of habitual thought and practices. Rather than being called to make sense of the events, to code and categorize, the photo essay invites a reimagining of bodies that are less boundaried and understood as connected to place, space, actions and ethical becomings. The chapter concludes by posing a difficult set of questions: how might these photographs create otherwise political and ethical action in early childhood education? How might they turn normalized gendered categorizations inside out and upside down? How might they become possibilities for challenging the 'perils of visibility' (Alaimo, 2010b: 23)?

This book pays homage to decades of groundbreaking feminist research that has been undertaken in early childhood contexts and has pushed debates and conceptualizations of children, childhood and gender in significant directions. The collection of chapters in this book underscores the persistent need to stay concerned by the small stuff that unfolds in the lives of women and children. The spaces, places and materialities that shape and inflect the world of early childhood have much to tell us if only we are prepared to listen, to grapple, to embrace uncertainty in our investigations and to be open to what else might be there. It is the extraordinary in early childhood that makes it a queer space overflowing with abundant opportunities for researchers to immerse themselves with the world-making practices that are undertaken every day as part of seemingly unremarkable rituals, practices, encounters, entanglements or what Stewart (2007: 2) recognizes as ordinary happenings: 'they're things that happen. They happen in impulses, sensations, expectations, daydreams, encounters, and habits of relating, in strategies and their failures, in forms of persuasion, contagion, and compulsion, in modes of attention, attachment and agency, and in publics and social worlds of all kinds that catch people up in something that feels like *some*thing'. She goes on to stress that 'they work not through meanings per se, but rather through bodies, dreams, dramas, and social worldlings of all kinds. Their significance lies in the intensities they build and what thoughts and feelings they make possible'.

This book has sought to attend to our situated knowledges (Haraway, 1988) as sentient beings, entangled in the queer spaces of early childhood that insist upon a deep concern with the everydayness of childhoods. Attention to the 'somethings' that arrest our attention within the routine, habitual and often seemingly unremarkable has informed the shape that this book (as both processes of becoming and as material thing) has taken on.

2

Re-turns and Dis/continuities of Feminist Thought in Childhood Research: Indebtedness and Entanglements

Jayne Osgood and Kerry H. Robinson

This chapter aims to map some examples of key feminist philosophies, theories and research that have shaped understandings of childhood and gender in significant ways in the recent past. It attends to important shifts over time, but it does not argue for chronology or linearity; rather the aim is to illuminate how a rich tapestry of feminist thought has been activated and practised through research to generate important ruptures to established ways of thinking about children and gender. By reviewing what has come before, we identify how previous feminist scholarship leaves traces and, in many senses, shapes the exciting research that is being undertaken in the field of childhood studies by feminist researchers currently. We want to celebrate the important contributions that feminist philosophers and scholars have made to the field and to explore the possibilities that are opened for feminist new materialists to work with ideas about gender and childhood generatively but in ways that recognize their indebtedness to the past.

The fundamental purpose of this chapter is to identify the centrality of feminism and feminist thought to the field of early childhood studies and the continued relevance of gender to all debates about childhood. This entails an engagement with the affordances that feminist theory has created to conceptualize the child and childhood in ways that challenge dominant conservative and regressive ideas, policies and practices. Furthermore, the chapter considers how feminist scholars of childhood have taken up post-structuralist and queer theory to further extend understandings of gender and sexuality. The significance of this work to generating more equitable and transformative pedagogies in early childhood education is also considered.

Starting in the middle ...

We take the 1980s as an interesting entry point into considering how feminist and LGBTQI+ communities generated an important rupture that offered re-conceptualizations of gender, sexuality and childhood in early childhood studies. Globally, the 1980s was an important decade politically, socially, economically and environmentally. It was an era shaped by global commitments to neo-liberalism, an economic ideology based on promoting rational self-interest through processes of privatization, deregulation, globalization and tax cuts, in a global environment of increasing threats of nuclear war, as a result of Cold War politics. The politics of the 'new right' were inherently conservative and framed by a concern with the neo-liberal subject. It was also a period in which micro politics were demanding the attention of the global, asserting what happens in the local, particularly environmentally, significantly impacts all of us as global citizens and future generations.

In the UK, the British prime minister of the time, Margaret Thatcher, was a central figure in global politics committed to neo-liberalism. As the first female prime minister, she became known as the 'Iron Lady'; the philosophy of monetarism underpinned her policies which were uncompromising and had far-reaching consequences for social justice, equality and education (David, 1992). The implementation of inherently masculinist policies though relied upon gendered tropes, she claimed to be running the nation's budget like 'a thrifty housewife'. She also appropriated the 'personal is political' mantra of second-wave feminists, stressing the significance of her working-class background and status as a working mother. These classed and gendered subjectivities were fundamental to the image she projected to the electorate, which further symbolically stressed that success is possible for anyone but that it is reliant upon individual hard work: that is the enterprising neo-liberal subject. Thatcher was also a staunch advocate of traditional family values, hailing them as the only way to improve society. It was through the traditional, heteronormative nuclear family that individual subjects would become economically successful and aspire to middle-class sensibilities (Arnot & Barton, 1992). Within this vision, conventional marriages and nuclear families were considered the fundamental building blocks to a successful nation. An important example of this was the inclusion of Section 28 of the Local Government Act 1988. This controversial clause stated that a local authority shall not 'promote the teaching in any maintained school of the acceptability of homosexuality as a pretended family relationship'. The Conservative government, under Margaret Thatcher, introduced some of the most regressive reforms to the education system, which reignited social class divisions and exacerbated inequalities (Gewirtz et al., 1995).

LGBTQI+ and feminist groups were among some of the most active and vociferous against Thatcherism as an ideology and a set of politics. Neo-liberalism, the New Right and Thatcherism were all working to effectively dismantle and threaten many of the ideological and political advances that had been gained by the New Social Movements throughout the 1960s and 1970s (Hall, 1988). On 5 September 1981, female protesters descended upon RAF Greenham Common in the south of England to challenge the political decision reached by the Thatcher and Reagan administrations, to site ninety-six cruise missiles on the RAF base. The women presented a letter to the base commander stating: 'We fear for the future of all our children and for the future of the living world which is the basis of all life.'

The Greenham Common Peace protest was notable for many reasons, but the fact that it was a peaceful, women-only protest is significant:

> Greenham was a place where a generation of women found a public voice. It was a voice that was predicated on inclusion and difference, multiple perspectives not a single dominant view. It identified earlier than most that we had been let down by a political class, that the interests of ordinary people had been ignored in favour of warmongers and international business interests. (*The Guardian*, 2013)

Image 2.1 Body politics. Source: https://www.telegraph.co.uk/news/politics/margaret-thatcher/10213479/Thatcher-said-Greenham-Common-anti-nuclear-protesters-were-an-eccentricity.html

The media reported that protestors were predominantly heterosexual women, using their maternal subjectivities as grounds for protest against nuclear weapons in the name of safeguarding their children and future generations. The women-only protestors were making a very public statement; refusal to go home at the end of each day of protest was a direct challenge against traditional conjugal roles. However, the protestors came under a barrage of attack from politicians, media and local residents, all variously claiming that being at home, caring for their children, would be greater proof of their maternal convictions.

The Greenham Common Protest lasted over twenty years and continues to provide a focus for debate among feminists (Shepherd, 2014). In debates about childhood, gender and sexuality, the Greenham Peace Camp is of particular interest (Kidron, 2007). The ways in which the women peacefully mobilized, agitated and persisted in pursuit of social justice provide an important contrast to global and national politics of the time:

> Everything, from how to allocate donations to the distribution of cooking rotas was democratically decided … the women worked out how to care for the young, how to humiliate the authorities on the ground while arguing the case in the highest courts of the land, how to live with difference while living in a community that claimed one thing – the decommissioning of nuclear weapons – was more important than all other considerations. (*The Guardian*, 2013)

Shepherd (2014) argues that the Greenham Common Peace movement took 'the child' as metaphor and physical embodiment of vulnerability to inform the politics that were enacted through women-only protest. The protest raised questions about boundaries; these women self-consciously transgressed metaphorical and physical boundaries and used these transgressions to frame their protest. They were pushing against gendered tropes about what it is to be a woman and what it is to be a mother. In many senses, their female bodies became a carefully choreographed statement of collective feminist agency. Furthermore, the spatial context of the peace camp was itself liminal; mothers had left fixed houses for temporary and uncertain settlements on common land; they had transported female (and in some cases their children's) bodies into public space in a confrontational quest to trouble what else 'home' and 'security' might mean. The protest sent powerful, disruptive messages that challenged hegemonic discourses about family, gender, environment, power and politics. This challenge was 'voiced' through the arrangements of human bodies and the materialized enactments of protest. For example, toys and nappies (symbols of humdrum domesticity) were physically attached to the cold, barbed wire, perimeter fence shadowed by the nuclear missile silos. These domesticated materials mattered: they contrasted to the high-powered, international politics of the nuclear base. They mattered because they symbolized idealized motherhood and offered a culturally intelligible narrative: one of maternal protection. This protest was met with disdain; for example Young (1990: 2) claimed it was 'criminal activity, a witches' coven, a threat to the state, the family and the democratic order'.

Similarly, as part of the international feminist peace movement, 700 women, on 11 November (Remembrance Day) 1983, led by a delegation of local and non-local Indigenous women, marched on the Pine Gap Defence Facility near Alice Springs in the central desert region of Australia. This US military base was established in 1970 as part of a treaty between the United States and Australian government stemming from fears of Cold War threats and the invention of cruise missiles. The women-only protesters set up the Pine Gap Women's Peace Camp at the gates of the military facility, where they remained for two weeks, temporarily making this Space Base 'uncannily homely' (Bartlet, 2013). Historically, the Australian desert has been the preferred location of military test sites with Pine Gap not that far from the Woomera Rocket Range and Maralinga, used as a nuclear test site by the British government in the 1950s and 1960s. The impact of atomic testing at Maralinga has had immeasurable impact on Aboriginal communities, including children, leading to displacement, injury and death (Tynan, 2016).

The Pine Gap Women's Peace Camp sang, danced and used graffiti, banners, artwork, mass silence and human bodies to not only attract national and international media attention around their cause but also challenge white masculinist discourses of authority and power, underpinning Western colonialist and imperialist government policies of the time. The Boston Tea Party, as it was called, was central to the women's planned political actions. On 13 November, 111 women chose to climb over the gates, helped by other women who formed a human pyramid to support the climb. Once over the gate, the women staged a picnic on the lawns, pitching umbrellas and laying down blankets and food. As each woman was arrested, they gave their name as Karen Silkwood, the US anti-nuclear campaigner, who died in a suspicious car accident on the same day nine years earlier (Bartlet, 2013).

Both Greenham Common and the Pine Gap Women's Peace Camp are examples of performances of body politics interrupting global politics in small but significant ways; these female bodies mattered in global politics and generated both affects and effects; they produce and are produced by political practices that intervene on a global scale. Following Butler (*Bodies That*

Matter), Shepherd (2014) asks how is it that some performances of gender are congruent with, or disruptive of, the limits of intelligibility in a given cultural context? These examples of the international Women's Peace Movement were viewed as threatening because they transgressed appropriate behavioural limits (neglecting maternal caring responsibilities, absent from the family home) in spectacularly mundane ways (forming human chains, dancing on silos, attaching nappies and toys to fences). They were represented in media coverage as: 'threatening to family values at best, and at worst as providing a sanctuary for lesbians, one-parent families and lost causes' (Newbury resident quoted in *The Daily Mail*, cited in Cresswell, 1994: 50). A key political feature in both cases was overturning the heteronormativity of place and authority. In the context of Pine Gap, Australian feminist theorist Alison Bartlet comments:

> The masculine authority invested in understandings of the military and the desert was challenged by the visibly women-only protest, as the heterosexual matrix was threatened by the visibly lesbian protesters. (2013: 922)

The global LGBTQI+ movement has also played a leading role in challenging heteronormative understandings of gender, sexuality, family and childhood; opening up opportunities for doing gender, sexuality and family differently; pushing for equal rights and critical law reforms such as the decriminalization of homosexuality; and increasing awareness of the violence experienced by LGBTQI+ people, as well as other impacts of transphobia and homophobia on their lives. It was not until 1992 that the World Health Organization declassified same-sex attraction as a mental illness. The consequent riots (fighting back) erupting from brutal police attacks on transwomen, drag queens and gay men at the Gene Compton's Café in Tenderloin, San Francisco, in 1966, and the Stonewall Inn in New York City in 1969, are considered to mark the beginning of this international movement (Pasulka, 2015). The year 2018 marks the forty year anniversary of the Gay and Lesbian Mardi Gras in Sydney, Australia. However, these festivities also emerged from brutal police attacks on a group of LGBTQI+ people in 1978 who peacefully marched and gathered in a public space to commemorate the Stonewall riots, to protest against discrimination and oppression, and to celebrate their lives – a merging of discourse and bodies. Fifty-three people were arrested that night after a violent confrontation with police. Although most of the charges were dropped, the names and addresses of those arrested appeared in a leading Sydney newspaper, outing them to friends, family and employers. Many lost their families, home and jobs as homosexuality was still a crime. Today, it is one of the largest events in the world attended by hundreds of thousands of people, bringing 38 million dollars annually to the Australian economy with more than 130 floats representing organizations supporting LGBTQI+ rights and celebrating LGBTQI+ communities – two of which are the New South Wales Police Force and Rainbow Families.

Body politics and the articulation of protest through materialized practices can be traced backwards to the peaceful protests of the suffragists and can also unfurl into contemporary feminist and LGBTQI+ movements such as the global Million Women Rise, Marriage Equality, and online campaigns such as #MeToo. The importance of the material, discursive, affective and corporeal threads through and entangles the past to the future via the present. Of course, feminist protests must not be viewed unproblematically; each of the aforementioned feminist movements has been critiqued on the grounds of exclusivity. In different cultural contexts, certain bodies are rendered more intelligible (on the basis of gender, sexuality, social class background, ethnicity and able-bodiedness, transgender and gender fluid bodies) than others. However, these examples of women-only, peaceful activist practices each offer materialized figurations of feminist collective resistances which create conditions to imagine alternative possibilities for children and women. Feminist protest witnesses the emergence of the past, present and future colliding in productive ways. Gender and childhood are central to these events, and the ideologies underpinning them concern collective resistance and, significantly, resistance that is realized through both materialized and embodied practices. This political context and these feminist activist practices are not separate from feminist scholarship and research. This chapter goes on to explore how the wider sociopolitical and cultural contexts in which children are located are productive of them as gendered subjects.

Frogs and snails and feminist tales

The deeply conservative political backdrop of the 1980s provided both context and motivation to undertake research about childhood and gender that could shift the hegemonic ideas circulating in political and media discourses. Since the 1980s, gender has increasingly been acknowledged as an important aspect of children's subjectivity to be addressed through early childhood research. This research has raised awareness and understandings of gendering processes in childhood and how these processes relate to the constitution of children as knowing, agentic subjects with a sense of themselves as gendered and sexual subjects (Davies, 1989; Greishaber, 1998; Thorne, 1993).

Feminist theorists have made significant contributions to how gender and childhood are thought about over the past thirty years; this shift in thinking has framed bodies of scholarship and research that continue to push debates and open up other lines of thought about what it means to be/do feminist research and how to engage children in that research in ways that recognize their contribution (e.g. Ringrose et al., 2015). Feminist scholars continue to be at the forefront of debates in this area, challenging long-established conceptualizations which locate ideas about gender principally within biological and developmentalist frameworks. Within these debates, feminist and queer scholars have unsettled the established idea that sexuality is only a matter of concern in adolescence and adulthood; instead they highlight the influence of sexuality norms on processes of doing gender from early childhood onwards.

Around the 1980s, feminist educational research was at pains to highlight that gender and sexuality in children's everyday lives are socially and culturally constructed. Feminist post-structuralist researchers shifted awareness about gender and sexuality by challenging the idea that children are passively engaged in sex-role socialization. Instead, this research highlighted that children are central to the construction of their own gender and sexual subjectivities and, furthermore, to the regulation and policing of gender and sexuality norms of both children and adults around them. From very early ages, children start to explore gendered and sexual identities from accounts and narratives offered by family, educators, peers and via the media about what it means to be a girl or a boy, a woman or a man. Queer theory has provided feminist post-structuralist researchers with the means to mobilize critical perspectives and so disrupt binary understandings of gender and heteronormative assumptions about latent (hetero)sexuality in childhood.

Despite decades of feminist scholarship that stresses gender is socially constructed through discourse, biological and developmentalist theories of gender difference persist in much early childhood education research and practice. The re-emergence of neuroscientific explanations for gender differences further reinforces the view that gender is hardwired into children. The media interest in, and perpetuation of, neuroscientific accounts is especially noteworthy, but so too is the lack of evidence underpinning such explanations that have been exposed by feminist scholars. Notwithstanding this conservativism and resistance to viewing gender as processual and fluid, there has been increased public awareness about gender as contingent, diverse and multiple. Transgender identities among young children have gained increasing attention from media, practitioners and researchers. The increasing numbers of children and young people openly identifying as gender diverse or transgender in recent times highlight the inadequacy and outdatedness of binarized thinking about gender, which fails to capture the complexity of the lived experiences of many young people. This gender shifting and fluidity poses some important questions for understanding the development of gender and gendered subjectivities in childhood, bringing debates about gender identity, discourse, bodies and power even more significantly to the fore.

By mapping feminist theorizing in early childhood throughout this chapter, it will become possible to expose the generative potential offered within studies of early childhood that have persistently reworked understandings of childhood and gender. Although there have been important shifts in how this has manifested, it also insists upon a re-turn to some of the intractable 'truths' that persist (about childhood innocence, developmentalism, biological determinism). Contemporary feminist perspectives point to the importance of considering the interrelationships between the sociocultural, the material and the affective when theorizing childhood. Attending to these interconnections presents possibilities for research methodologies to stretch understandings of gender as processual, fleeting and always becoming in early childhood. Feminist new materialism offers the potential to extend awareness of gender in early childhood education and to find ways to immerse researchers in practices that produce gender as sensed, felt, encountered through entangled processes of world-making. Like feminist post-structuralists, feminist new materialists are in the 'thick of things'; they claim neither objectivity nor impartiality. Feminist researchers have always recognized their subjective, partial and situated place in research (Haraway, 1988). Foregrounding how materiality and affect work in processes of producing gender presents a detour from capturing discursive accounts and re/presenting the performances of children as gendered subjects. It is our contention that both the material *and* discursive remain significant cornerstones to feminist thought in childhood research. As Barad (2003: 822) stresses:

> The relationship between the material and the discursive is one of mutual entailment. Neither is articulated/articulable in the absence of the other; matter and meaning are mutually articulated. Neither discursive practices nor material phenomena are ontologically or epistemologically prior. Neither can be explained in terms of the other. Neither has privileged status in determining the other.

Throughout this chapter, attention is paid to the ways in which feminist scholars have worked with the material, affective, corporeal and discursive to push ideas about gendered subjectivities, performances and processes.

Sugar and spice and all things nice, what are little girls made of?

Feminist scholars have shaped, and continue to shape, the field of gender studies, most significantly in the context of childhood. This has been primarily through a challenge to hegemonic discourses on gender differences framed by biological determinism. Biological determinism argues that gender difference is constituted within binarized understandings of gender, wherein males and females are 'natural' opposites. Biologically, male and female bodies, brains, sex hormones and genes are said to be diametrically opposite. The foundation of this argument is extended to account for differences in intellect, psychology and behaviour which are also argued to be biologically determined and ultimately considered the essence of masculinity and femininity. To be male is to be tough, robust, rational, daring, fearless, original, tenacious and mathematically and spatially inclined. By contrast, being female is claimed to be characterized by being reliant, submissive, sensitive, weak, emotional, irrational and fearful. Based on this hypothesis, girls and boys, women and men are considered to be 'naturally' predisposed to particular roles based on their sex and consequently channelled into disciplinary fields and occupational groups. Biological determinism was also used as both explanation and justification for the division of life into private and public spheres, with women generally relegated to the private domain of the home to take up caring responsibilities; while men were consigned to the public sphere to occupy positions of power and authority and to provide financial security for the family.

By the late 1960s through to the 1980s, biological determinist explanations for gender difference started to lack credibility and were critiqued on the grounds that they failed to take account of differences within gendered groups. Feminist scholars began to question the hegemonic discourse of biologically determined sex role differences, and so essentialism and the hegemony of biological explanations of gender came under scrutiny. For example, Money and Ehrhardt (1972) and Maccoby and Jacklin (1974) stressed that social factors were more significant than biology in the development of gender differences. Around the same time, feminist scholars challenged the 'naturalness' of psychological and behavioural differences by gender, claiming that differences could be attributed to processes of socialization through which children learnt what it meant to be a boy or a girl from their everyday experiences. How to enact gender was learnt through everyday messages transmitted from home, school and via the media. *The Psychology of Sex Differences* (Maccoby & Jacklin, 1974) made an important contribution to shifting debates by directly challenging the centrality of biological determinism used to explain gender differences. Furthermore, the authors were aligned to ideas put forward by intersectional feminists (Crenshaw, 1989; hooks, 1981) who pointed out that there are far greater differences within genders than between them.

Aligned to challenges from feminist research about how sex differences were explained, feminist theorists provided critiques of how biology had been put to work to justify gender inequalities. Feminists also highlighted the sexist perspectives that were generally inherent in scientific explanations that 'naturalized' gender differences (Haraway, 1989). The feminist and queer studies scholar de Lauretis (1987) in *Technologies of Gender: Essays on Theory, Film and Fiction* argued: 'Gender is not sex, a state of nature, but rather the representation of each individual in terms of a particular social relation which pre-exists the individual and is predicated on the conceptual and rigid (structural) opposition of two biological sexes' (p. 5). De Lauretis (1987) stressed that gender 'is always intimately interconnected with political and economic factors in society … [and] systematically linked to the organization of social inequality' (p. 5). Feminist researchers provided a powerful analysis of the way that everyday practices of dressing children in gender-stereotyped clothes; buying gender-stereotyped toys; the perpetuation of gender stereotypes in advertisements, songs, television, games, books and magazines; and children's gender-stereotyped play and interactions were central to constructing gender differences around biological sex. Alice Honig (1983) argued that by the age of four, gender influenced children's play preferences, behaviour and social expectations of themselves and others. Echoing the earlier words of the feminist theorist Simone de Beauvoir (1949), the educational researcher Barrie Thorne (1993) pointed out, 'if boys and girls are different, they are not born but *made* that way' (p. 2).

Schooling was also recognized as an important site where gender socialization occurred and sex role inequalities were exacerbated. Hence, a wave of feminist research located in school classrooms and playgrounds emerged in the 1980s to explore how gendered inequalities manifested and their effects. Askew and Ross (1988), Browne and France (1986), and Honig (1983) drew upon reproduction theory to account for gender differences. The thesis being that inequalities are reproduced by children based upon the ways that adults (namely parents and teachers) reinforce traditional stereotypes through gendered behaviours and unequal engagements with boys and girls (which continue to persist today, as evidenced in a documentary aired in the UK, BBC, 2017). Of special interest to the research in the 1980s were children's books, teaching materials and school curricula. An examination of these texts and how they were put to work by teachers revealed disturbing gendered pedagogical practices that routinely privileged boys over girls. Boys were afforded more attention in classroom, and gender differences and associated inequalities were habitually reinforced.

Feminist research within the classroom identified sexism across all educational phases, including the early years. Early childhood teachers took up taken-for-granted ideas about gender underpinned by essentialism and biological determinism. Gendered play in nursery classrooms tended to be attributed to children's 'natural' predispositions – that is, that girls were instinctively drawn to dolls and home corner, while boys naturally gravitate towards more physical, risk-taking activities. Children's books tended to emphasize sex role differences, with male protagonists typically engaged in gendered pursuits. The logic being that if boys could identify with a (gendered) character like themselves, the disinterest that many boys show towards reading could be addressed.

Ain't I a Woman ...

> We, black women who advocate feminist ideology, are pioneers. We are clearing
> a path for ourselves and our sisters. We hope that as they see us reach our goal –
> no longer victimized, no longer unrecognized, no longer afraid – they will take
> courage and follow. (hooks, 1982: 196)

This quote from black feminist, bell hooks, underlines a significant flaw in second-wave feminism and in childhood research undertaken at the same time. hooks was among a body of black feminist scholars to critique feminist thought for failing to acknowledge how gender intersects with other aspects of identity or multiple subjectivities such as sexuality, ethnicity, social class background and able-bodiedness. Feminist theorists such as Kimberle Crenshaw (1989), Audre Lorde (1984) and bell hooks (1984) stressed that much feminist theory was saturated with white, middle-class values and experiences, which fundamentally failed to connect to the experiences of black women; second-wave feminism was found wanting for the exclusionary culture and practices it perpetuated. Black feminists stressed that oppression, victimization and exclusion experienced by black women were profoundly different to that experienced by white middle-class women. Black women's experiences of oppression were primarily shaped by processes of marginalization generated from racism – with patriarchy a very real but secondary form of oppression. As the opening quote from hooks stresses, white middle-class feminists were implicit in perpetuating oppression for black women through their racist practices and privileged position in society, so much so that for the majority of black women, feminism seemed to have nothing relevant to offer. The works of Lorde and hooks and other theorists, such as Mohanty (1991), provided a pressing reminder that social inequalities and abuses of power must be understood through a framework of intersectionality. Working to ensure that difficult differences, such as race, ethnicity and cultural heritage, enter into feminist activism (and scholarship) represented a significant moment that altered the shape of childhood, gender and sexualities research. Feminist researchers were required to become more attuned to whose knowledge becomes 'truth' and whose knowledge is written out of history or social experiences. This has been significant within the field of early childhood studies where gendered experiences for children from culturally and linguistically diverse backgrounds are addressed more attentively. For example, Cannella and Viruru (2004) assess the powerful impression of colonialism in defining and viewing gender and childhood through Western discourses. Working with postcolonial theory, which is closely aligned to intersectionality, the authors (2004) stress that:

> Discourses of racial difference (and superiority) have also been predicated on beliefs about gender; racism and sexism have become so intertwined that they are impossible to separate. (p. 42)

Furthermore, 'Gender is a false truth that has been used by some European and American males (and others who accept the notions as beyond question) to impose patriarchy, racism, and control on indigenous and other colonized people' (p. 43).

Recognizing gender as socially constructed offered alternative discourses from which to provide explanations for how gendered identities are formed, to account for differences between and within the genders, and to provide accounts of the production and persistence of inequalities based upon gender.

Aboriginal women scholars in Australia (Langton, 1998; Martin, 2008) highlighted their concerns about how Indigenous voices and Indigenous knowledge systems had for 'too long lain buried beneath the overwhelming dominance of the only voice permitted, the voice that continually represents the western knowledge system as the only legitimate truth' (Herbert, 2005: 2). Aboriginal education scholar Jeannie Herbert (2005: 3) argued that historical perceptions of Indigenous Australians of non-Indigenous Australians as 'not belonging' or 'not having a place' in education systems that valued Western knowledge and epistemologies only resulted in their exclusion and oppression, even of those Aboriginal people who were 'successful' within Western education communities. Within a context of individual and institutional racism, epitomized, for example, by government colonialist 'protection' policies of the 1860s–1940s, Indigenous Australians have had to negotiate education systems and educators, who were core to the implementation of such policies. These policies led to the dispossession – loss of land, culture, histories, languages and identity – experienced by Aboriginal peoples and have been foundational to the inequities they experience in contemporary Australian society (Fforde etal., 2013; Herbert, 2005; Langton, 1998; Lippmann, 1994; Moreton-Robinson, 2009, 2017).

Aileen Moreton-Robinson (2017) points out that Indigenous people's sense of belonging stems from an ontological relationship to country based on the Dreaming – what is believed to have occurred at the beginning in the original form of social living created by ancestral beings. Moreton-Robinson (2017, npn) goes on to say:

> Ancestral beings changed form and gender, and in many cases are associated with elements or natural species … Because the ancestral spirits gave birth to humans, they share a common life force, which emphasizes *the unity of humans with the earth rather than their separation* … The ontological relationship occurs through inter-substantiation of ancestral beings, humans and land – it is a form of *embodiment.*

Life history narratives of Australian Indigenous women in the 1980s and 1990s were framed within their experiences of being removed from their families and country of origin and on collective memories of intergenerational relationships primarily between indigenous women, extended families and communities. Foundational to these relationships are connections between country and the spirit world. Core to all the life narratives is that all indigenous people are related by descent, country, place or shared experiences (Moreton-Robinson, 2017). 'Indigenous women', Moreton-Robinson comments, 'perceive themselves as being an extension of the earth, which is alive and unpredictable'. The life histories of Indigenous women, Moreton-Robinson (2017, npn) says:

> show a moral ordering of sociality which emphasises mutual support and concern for those with whom they are interconnected. Their ontological relationship to home and place facilitates this connectedness and belonging. While this ontology is omnipresent it is rarely visible, often elusive and most often unrecognisable for many non-Indigenous people in their inter-subjective relations with Indigenous people.

As highlighted in this discussion, Indigenous knowledge systems (or meaning making) are a combination of the discursive, the material and the affective –

an intimate relationship between synthesizing the oral, written, images, the material and sensing the spiritual (Martin, 2008). Of particular importance to Indigenous intellectual traditions and inquiry are ethical relationships. As Eve Tuck and Marcia McKenzie (2015a: 10) argue there is a long history of indigenous peoples 'being subjected to unethical researchers and the unethical ways in which Indigenous materials, samples, stories and intellectual property have been improperly handled and dispersed in academe'. Decolonizing perspectives informed by Indigenous perspectives aim to address the real and symbolic violence inherent in colonialism (Tuck and McKenzie, 2015a).

Gender trouble: Feminism and the subversion of identity

This section borrows the title from Judith Butler's 1990 book which so perfectly captures the epistemological shift in feminist theorizing which recognized children as far more agentic and capable than either reproduction or socialization theories allowed for. The work of Judith Butler was enormously influential in childhood studies of gender, highlighting understandings of how children perform and produce gender in sophisticated ways. During the 1990s, research into gender in childhood was shaped by feminist post-structuralism that reconceptualized gender in childhood as socially, culturally and discursively constructed (Davies, 1989; Greishaber, 1998; MacNaughton, 2000; Walkerdine, 1990). Underpinning this feminist work were the philosophies of radical thinkers such as Foucault (knowledge and power), Butler (gender performativity) and Derrida (deconstruction). Drawing upon and putting to work these concepts enabled feminist post-structuralists to account for gendered subjectivities as multiple, contradictory and shifting. Furthermore, these feminist scholars insisted that children must be understood as embedded within relations of power and actively exercising agency, hence the 'subversion of identity' that Butler argues for, which allows for children to actively take up or resist gendered subjectivities.

Shifting the focus to children as agentic and actively producing gender marked a significant epistemological shift in childhood studies. Through processes of deconstruction, feminist scholars were enabled to investigate how children make sense of themselves as gendered beings, as positioned as certain sorts of subjects within the cultural discourses of gender available to them (which are inflected with age, sexuality, social class background and ethnicity), and make certain gendered subjectivities more intelligible for some children than others. Feminist post-structuralists exposed the limitations of sex role and socialization theories for the lack of agency it afforded children. Within these conceptualizations of how gender is produced, children are constructed as passive recipients and entirely inactive in processes of gender formation (Cannella, 1997; Davies, 1989; Robinson & Jones-Diaz, 2006). Bronwyn Davies (1989) argued: 'These theories [socialization and sex role theory] of the person obscure our recognition of the complex and contradictory ways in which we are continually constituting and reconstituting ourselves and the social world through the various discourses in which we participate' (p. 6). Aristotelian ideas of children as 'tabula rasa' are refuted by feminist post-structuralists; instead they argue that children actively negotiate, resist, constitute and perpetuate the cultural narratives of 'appropriate' and 'correct' gender performances of being male or female.

For feminist post-structuralists, binarized gender categories are unstable and contested social categories. These categories are infused with meanings and representations that shift, slide and mutate across and within different cultures over time. These scholars have highlighted the multiple ways in which masculinities and femininities are performed within and across cultures, challenging antiquated fixed and universalized understandings of binarized gender. Judith Butler's (1990, 1994) account of performativity of gender argues that it is through the process of iteration that the individual gendered subject comes into being. For Butler, iteration is the regularized and constrained repetition of norms and it is through this process that identities are constituted and others excluded. It is also through this process of iteration that differences occur resulting in change. Through acknowledging the performative, relational and discursive nature of gender, feminist post-structuralist scholars have shown how change becomes possible. This understanding of gender as dynamic and open to change through processes and performances provided the foundation for feminist new materialists to extend on these ideas. Karen Barad, for example, provides a different understanding of performativity through a post-humanist lens based on iterative intra-activity, rather than iterative citationality as in Butler's theorization of performativity (Barad, 2003). Butler's and Barad's different readings of performativity are discussed further in Chapter 3. West and Zimmerman (1987: 140) view gender as an 'accomplishment' pointing out that 'sex category and gender are managed properties of conduct that are contrived with respect to the fact that others will judge and respond to us in particular ways ... gender is not simply an aspect of what one is, but, more fundamentally, it is something that one does, and does recurrently, in interaction with others'. Assumptions of heteronormativity have permeated theories of child development, and gender stereotypes have remained constant, despite increased flexibility in adult social roles, the greater visibility of lesbian and gay adults, and the increasing awareness of gender diverse and transgender children and young people.

Transgender scholars have differing views about gender diverse and transgender identities. Susan Stryker (2008), for example, argues that people with transgender identities can describe themselves as men or women or resist binary categorization, but either way they still queer and challenge the dominant relationship of the sexed body and gendered subject. However, Jay Prosser (2013: 56) maintains that transsexuality is a move from one recognizable sex category to the other, that the material body (the flesh) is important to the self and that 'the desire to pass as "really gendered" in the world without trouble' is crucial to transsexual subjects.

Research dealing with gender diverse and transgender children and young people has tended to focus broadly on LGBTQI+ issues and experiences. The 'No Outsiders' project in the UK (2006–2008) focused on the inclusive pedagogical practices of fifteen primary school teachers who promoted LGBTQI+ equality (Greytak et.al., 2009). An important outcome of this research was that younger children were perceived to be ready to deal with gender and sexuality issues challenging the discourses that prevail around childhood and sexuality. Much of the educational research focuses on developing teaching resources/guide books for working with gender and sexuality diverse students based on teachers' experiences and challenging heteronormativity in schools through school policies, teacher pedagogies and curricula changes (García & Slesaransky-Poe, 2010; Jarvis & Sandretto, 2010). Research on gender diversity and transgender identities in early childhood (aged 0–5) is rare and tends to be framed in terms of building inclusive school environments for LGBTQI+ families in early childhood settings (Burt et al., 2010).

Wonder within the queerness of childhood

The important work of feminist post-structuralists outlined above pushed conceptualizations of children and childhood in exciting new directions. Recognizing children as agentic beings, navigating discourses and negotiating gendered identities was a crucial step in reassessing childhood and the need for different modes of engaging with children through research and pedagogical practices. This important body of scholarship has made a considerable impression on the public psyche that is now generally more willing to view children as active citizens contributing to the social, economic and political worlds of which they form part and the sense-making they undertake about themselves as gendered (classed, raced, etc.) subjects. Meanwhile though, sexuality in early childhood education remains a highly contentious and contested issue. While there is growing recognition, acknowledgement and acceptance of diverse family formations, including same-sex parents, sexuality is generally deemed a taboo irrelevance to children. The work of feminist scholars applying queer theory to studies of childhood represents an important rupture to this taken-for-granted assumption about children. Through research, the means by which children form sexuality identities, and the relationship this has with gendered identities, and ultimately the influence of children's early education on this process have been the subject of investigation (Blaise, 2010; Epstein, 1995; Goldman & Goldman, 1982; Renold, 2005; Robinson, 2005, 2013; Robinson & Davies, 2008b, 2010, 2015; Schwartz & Cappello, 2001).

Central to this body of work is Butler's concept of the heterosexual matrix (Butler, 1990) which argues that 'natural' and 'normalized' bodies, genders and desires are rendered culturally intelligible through processes of heterosexualization. Robinson (2013) argued that heterosexuality and heterosexual desire is a routine, everyday occurrence in childhood that goes largely unnoticed. Research with young children by feminist queer scholars (Blaise, 2005a, b; Renold, 2005; Robinson, 2013; Robinson & Davies, 2008b, 2010, 2015) reveals that children's understandings of sexuality and sexual identity are largely constituted through heteronormative discourses of gender. These scholars extend ideas that play is a significant site of gender construction in early childhood by arguing that it also provides space in which heteronormative discourses prevail. For example, the fantasy play that children engage in through mock weddings, families, kiss chase and so on forms part of children's heteronormative play narratives. However, these activities are dismissed as being linked to children's early sexuality formation; instead, educators and adults more generally argue that 'children are just being children' and that such games are a 'natural' aspect of 'normal' childhood development.

The studies into children's sexuality outlined here represent another significant rupture in the field of (feminist) studies of childhood. This scholarship has set the foundation to recognize and grapple with the queerness of childhood and the complex worlds in which children subvert, explore, transgress, conform and self-discipline against the material-discursive possibilities available to them. Recognizing the enormous, all pervading effect of heteronormativity discourses, and the material practices in early childhood contexts, raises a set of important questions about how children, educators, environments and materials shape embodied experiences and expressions of gender and sexuality that we go on to explore in subsequent chapters.

How gender comes to matter …

As this chapter attests, approaches taken to the study of gender in childhood to a large extent rest upon how children are conceptualized and the prevailing orthodoxies of the time, and the need to find alternative (feminist) narratives and ways in which to account for complexity and contradiction. The material and affective turns in the disciplinary fields of the social sciences and humanities urge that to better understand our (human) place within the world, we need to extend upon practices of identifying discourses and capturing representations (in this case of gender in early childhood) to producing different/other knowledges and more liveable worlds (Haraway, 2016). Hughes are Lury (2013) are among many feminist scholars to debate the challenges involved in engaging in new materialist and post-humanist research practices. They highlight the persistence of long-standing feminist concerns with positionality, relationality and interdisciplinarity; with what can be known and who can be a knower; and with the centrality of ethical, transformative practices within relations of power, as well as the acknowledgement that we live in, and are of, a more-and-other-than-human world. They argue that we must *re-turn* to one of the most significant concepts in feminist epistemology – that of situated knowledge or situatedness – but in such a way that takes account of how '"the human" is no less a subject of ongoing co-fabrication than any other socio-material assemblage' (Whatmore, 2006: 603 cited in Hughes & Lury, 2013).

The recent growth in feminist new materialist studies into aspects of childhood, including gender and sexuality, has variously taken up the challenge set out by Hughes and Lury (2013). The experimental approaches to researching gender in early childhood, mobilized by Huuki and Renold (2015), Osgood (2014, 2018), Jones (2013) and Lyttleton-Smith (2017) among others, recognize the indebtedness to a rich tapestry of feminist activism, philosophy and scholarship, much of which is set out in this chapter, but these new materialist feminists are endeavouring to generate new knowledge and to challenge some of the old orthodoxies that surround research practices. Taking up experimental approaches, framed by post-humanist and feminist new materialist theories and methods, extends some of the ideas and approaches taken up by feminist post-structuralists outlined earlier.

This growing body of early childhood research has been influenced by the work of philosophers working in other disciplinary fields (notably science studies) but who are similarly, deeply committed to feminist endeavours to reassess anthropocentric accounts of the child's place within the world. Specifically, Haraway, Barad and Braidotti have been influential feminist philosophers, who through their scholarship provide the means by which research can produce ways to extend understandings about gender in early childhood that attend to corporeal, material-discursive, intra-active processes of becoming. Bringing feminist new materialist philosophy to bear has allowed a re-engagement with postmodernist discourses and a fresh consideration of how gender in early childhood comes about through everyday, mundane, habitual events that are materially and discursively produced. Haraway (1994: 59) suggests that 'the point is to get at how worlds are made and unmade, in order to participate in the processes, in order to foster some forms of life and not others'. Her contention is that the feminist researcher has to recognize herself as engaged in world-making practices; through research with young children, the feminist researcher is embedded, entangled, infected and affected by the research context and all its (human and non-human) participants. Haraway (2016) invites researchers to engage in deep thoughtfulness and to become wayfarers and to work towards generating (other) stories. This mode of enquiry demands that feminist researchers persistently grapple with mundane, habitual, everyday occurrences. By attending to the everyday, it becomes possible to sense gender as emergent and constantly subject to change in sometimes predictable, and at other times unanticipated, ways. Through heightened ethical responsibility within research encounters, feminist researchers come to recognize and celebrate that human and the more-than-human relationalities are produced through 'worldling practices' (Haraway, 2016).

A growing number of feminist researchers are working with post-humanist logic to revisit and reconfigure understandings of gender in early childhood contexts by paying closer attention to materiality and affect through processes of becoming. Working with post-humanist and feminist new materialist theories has presented opportunities to think beyond the human subject (e.g. Lenz-Taguchi, 2010; Jones, 2013; Lyttleton-Smith, 2017). Working with flattened ontologies insists that the human subject is not privileged within any investigation, instead researchers are required to pay equal attention to materiality, affect, and corporeality. This confederate approach shifts the emphasis from viewing gender as an exclusively human concern to appreciating it as endlessly produced and reworked through entanglements; gender is generated through micro-events and is constantly shifting and mutating. This relatively recent concern with how corporeal, material and affective aspects of lives lived can produce new knowledges about gender in Early Childhood Education and Care (ECEC) contexts offers another rupture in feminist thought – a stutter that forces fresh consideration for how the child is conceptualized and understood as the 'posthuman child' (Murris, 2017).

Feminist new materialism insists that children and childhood be reconceptualized so that renewed attention is paid to early childhood pedagogies and research practices which can (re)consider how gendering processes are infinitely playing out and with what effects (Anastasiou, 2018; Lyttleton-Smith, 2017). The queerness of early childhood has been noted by feminist scholars for some time (Blaise, 2005a; Osgood, 2013, 2018; Robinson, 2005, 2013, 2008; Taylor, 2013). Very young children engage with the world in curious and unpredictable ways and have much to teach adults about our (human) place in the world. With a heightened attention to children's bodily place in early childhood contexts, feminist new materialism invites researchers to immerse themselves in the material-discursive entanglements that shape practice and to be attuned to the means by which children resist, challenge, indulge and transgress gendered ways of becoming through their inter- and intra-actions with human (e.g. peers, parents, educators), non-human (e.g. material, animal) and the more-than-human (e.g. computers). Attending to the verbal, non-verbal and physical enactments of gender in the routine unfolding of everyday life in childhood can produce surprising knowledge (Anastasiou, 2018; Holford, et al., 2013; Lyttleton-Smith, 2017; Osgood, 2018; Renold & Huuki, 2015). Reconfiguring knowledge about early childhood requires that researchers rethink thought (Holmes et al., 2018) and break free from established ideas about gender in early childhood. By resisting the temptation of viewing ourselves as expert knowers about children makes space for alternative knowledges to be produced. Developmentalist discourse is predicated on the idea that we can/do 'know' the child, and when a child (whom we think we know) is lacking against normative expectations, then, as expert knowers, it is our duty to fix that child (Blaise, 2013). Post-humanist decentring approaches set us free from this preoccupation so that we might pursue ideas that the child is variously and constantly interwoven within particular entanglements (Davies, 2014). In doing this, ways are offered to understand *gendering processes* in early childhood rather than to view the child as inherently gendered or reworking a gendered subjectivity.

Research in this paradigm attends to microscopic, multisensory investigations into relational entanglements of people, sensations, sounds, tastes, smells and matter. Early childhood is readily characterized by highly physical, emotional, unpredictable and seemingly chaotic encounters and so lends itself well to this mode of enquiry. This offers the feminist researcher infinite possibilities to turn attention to inter- and intra-actions forms of noise, smell, touch and to consider how such entanglements might inform our grapplings for new understandings of gendering processes (Jones, 2013; Osgood, 2018). The practical implication of post-humanist approaches to studying gender in ECEC is that they allow for a recognition of identities as generated relationally with objects, spaces and places and they are multisensory becomings that constantly mutate and transmute – making certainties about gender infinitely uncertain. Those who have taken this approach (Blaise, 2013a; Huuki & Renold, 2015; Lyttleton-Smith, 2015; Osgood, 2014, 2015a; Renold & Mellor, 2013;) have provided powerful illustrations of how the becoming child in early childhood contexts reworks and negotiates ways of being and transgressing what is thought knowable, doable, acceptable for little girls and boys (see Chapter 4).

While such approaches might be criticized for obscuring wider debates about gender and childhood (i.e. heteronormativity, misogyny, and how gender intersects with social class, ethnicity, disability and age), important investments have been made to ensure that these metanarratives remain in play when undertaking feminist new materialist research with young children. The wider stratified, social, political and economic contexts and the discursive production of inequalities and prejudices remain matters of concern to feminists working within this theoretical framework (Taylor et al., 2012). (See Chapter 4 for further discussion of these issues with prominent feminist theorists researching in early childhood.) However, it requires that researchers are prepared to be surprised, to question their worldviews and to consider afresh the interconnections of such metanarratives as they play out in and through the micropolitics and material-semiotic entanglements within early childhood contexts.

Working with post-humanist and new materialist approaches to examine gendering processes in early childhood creates opportunities to reconfigure established thought which makes it possible to find fissures within the hegemonic discourses that circulate within the media, curriculum frameworks, and research and pedagogical practices that can fix children as gendered subjects or mark them as deficient because they deviate from normative expectations of how to enact boy/girl. As we have claimed previously (Osgood & Robinson, 2016), offering children (and educators) the space to play with (gendering) processes of becoming is potentially liberating. Extending Butler's conceptualization of performativity to Barad's ideas is generative in the sense that it becomes possible to understand human subjectivity as always relationally generated through material-semiotic-affective assemblages – in which gender is constantly (re) produced.

Waves overlap at the same point in space

This chapter has attended to waves – waves of feminist activism, waves of feminist scholarship and waves of feminist research in early childhood education concerned to generate understandings about gender and sexualities. Attending to the movement of these waves, and specifically to overlaps, has exposed the generative project of feminist thought in childhood research. Through charting the waves, it is possible to discern the important contribution that feminist research has made to exposing, exploring and experimenting with ideas about gender in early childhood. It has underlined the significance of these contributions to the field and the vital political role that they play in refusing to allow gender to fall off the agenda. As Barad goes on to state:

> Diffraction has to do with the way waves combine when they overlap and the apparent bending and spreading of waves that occur when waves encounter an obstruction. … Under the right conditions, a diffraction pattern – a pattern of alternating light and dark lines – can be observed. (Barad, 2007: 74–75)

In *Generational Feminism* (2015), van der Tuin traces the diffractive patterns that have been productive in feminist thought. She challenges generational logic that argues that feminist theory and gender research is shaped by separatism between old and new approaches. She paves the way for a more complex notion of generationality, arguing that contemporary feminism is indebted to feminist foremothers and others yet to come. She opens up the concept 'generation' to argue for the connections between generations of feminists, as well as the generative potential of feminist thought to reimagine the feminist project. Building on generations of feminist epistemology can produce transversal moves and conceptual innovations that challenge conventional conceptions of space, time and mattering. Accounting for waves of feminist thought, as we have attempted to do in this chapter, and how they persistently interweave and reproduce is a significant undertaking but a productive one. We are in support of Barad's concept of dis/continuity (2012) that insists that we question assumptions about 'new' approaches to childhood studies concerned with gender. We challenge the notion that there must be some definitive cut with the past and instead argue for the importance of traces and entanglements. Our aim has been to offer a re-turning – which involves an openness to re-engage and re-immerse ourselves in the multiple projects of knowledge production that feminist scholars offer to the field. What this vast body of scholarship demonstrates is that gender remains a crucial aspect of all childhoods. Through convictions to problematize, critique, unsettle, map and reconfigure gender in early childhood, a long history of challenging what counts as valid knowledge (Lather, 1993) emerges. We urge that the field continues to interrogate who gets heard and what gets silenced or obscured from view in debates about gender and to consider deeply what queering dominant ideas about gender in early childhood research, theory and practice might afford us.

3

Re-turning Again: Dis/continuities and Theoretical Shifts in the Generational Generation of Discourses about Gender in Early Childhood Education

Kerry H. Robinson and Jayne Osgood

Introduction

As we have pointed out in the introductory chapter, this book is a research-based project exploring gender in early childhood and early childhood education, as well as examining what feminist theory, in its various iterations, has contributed to understandings in this area. The discussions across the chapters bring multiple academic voices and theoretical perspectives (e.g. feminist post-structuralism, feminist post-humanism, eco-feminism, queer theory and Marxist feminism). The chapters are also based on different research projects conducted with children, with early childhood educators and with gender theorists across different 'spacetimematterings', geolocations and political contexts. The research projects are based on a range of different methodologies – some may be considered post-qualitative (St. Pierre, 2017; St. Pierre & Jackson, 2014), while others have involved more traditional qualitative approaches. All the projects have brought a critical feminist political focus to the research. However, one of the main aims of this book has been to identify the strengths, connections, symmetries and tensions between feminist post-structuralism (FPS), which has been critical to furthering understandings of gender in early childhood over the past two decades or more, and feminist new materialism (FNM)/feminist post-humanism (FPH), which represents an emergent mode of enquiry into gender in childhood.

The discussion in this chapter is based on interviews with several prominent feminist scholars, at various stages of their academic careers, researching gender in early childhood, and who have made considerable contributions to understandings of gender in the field globally. These feminist scholars have also been influential in our own research into gender and sexuality over the years. Most of these scholars have had leading roles in the take-up or 'shift' to FNM/ FPH in early childhood, and others have been critical of that movement. In this project, we were interested to find out more about how these scholars perceived, understood and enacted the relationship between FPS and FNM/FPH, and the theoretical issues, concerns and movements they considered important to the apparent 'shift' in paradigm. In addition, we spoke to these scholars about the theoretical re-turns and dis/continuities they have experienced in their academic careers and the critical thinking behind these moves.

The interviews provided important insights into addressing gender in early childhood, as well as the theoretical movements in the careers of these feminist scholars, each of which is explored in this chapter. The interviews also demonstrated a shared perspective in terms of the perceived relationship between FPS and FNM/ FPH. The 'turn' to the ontological or FNM/FPH was not seen as a radical shifting away from FPS; indeed the relationship between the two theoretical perspectives was not considered antithetical but rather one viewed generally as a relationship of mutual benefit – one building and extending on the critical perspectives that each brings to epistemological and ontological understandings of the world and the intra-active and inter-active relationships between human, non-human and more-than-human; how they are constituted, situated and reconfigured; and how they overlap and entangle with each other across time, space, geolocation and political contexts.

Situating the project

The seeds of this book project were sown during numerous discussions, over several years, largely during conferences and periods of sabbatical in the UK and Australia. As we live on opposite sides of the globe (England and Australia), these physical face-to-face catch-ups were 'gold' and contrasted with the digitally material, technology-based, online catch-ups on which we have been reliant. The project stemmed from our mutual interest in feminist theory (in its various iterations), the influence of feminist theory in understanding gender in childhood and its impact on early childhood education curriculum and pedagogy (Osgood & Robinson, 2016). Our conversations over time raised many questions about the benefits and tensions associated with the 'shift' to FNM; what was potentially lost and gained through this movement; what was 'new' about these perspectives; whether FPS was actually already doing the work considered 'new' and different in FNM but just in different ways; and whether NM/PH were able to do the critical work in addressing diversity and difference, oppression and inequalities associated with aspects of identity (race, class, gender, sexuality, dis(ability) and so on). However, our most pressing question was whether the two theoretical paradigms could be used collaboratively to enhance the critical work that we do and lead more effectively to change. Primarily, we viewed this book project as an experiment in collaboration between FPS and FNM/FPH and a material-discursive openness to its unfolding in unpredictable ways.

Another central focus of our discussions was the question of whether gender had fallen off the early childhood agenda. Addressing gender equity and gender issues more generally within early childhood education tends to be met with varying degrees of commitment and perceptions of relevance and significance to children (Davies & Robinson, 2012; Robinson & Jones Diaz, 2000, 2006). Research conducted by Davies and Robinson (2012) with early childhood professionals in Australia echoed the findings of research conducted by Robinson and Jones Diaz (2000) more than a decade earlier. In both cases, the research highlighted the ambivalence of some early childhood professionals towards discussing gender issues with children – raising the question: to what extent has gender been a significant agenda item in early childhood education? Perceptions of more significant, pressing and relevant issues, such as 'behaviour management', disability, multiculturalism and bilingualism, continue to prevail in the field. Robinson (2013) argues that a hierarchy of difference generally underpins educators' (and many other professional contexts) perspectives of the importance and significance of addressing inequalities associated with different aspects of identity with children. This results in the pitting of different equity concerns against each other in the jostle for recognition in a time-poor environment with limited resources. This hierarchy of difference is also related to what educators feel more 'comfortable' addressing with children and their families. Gender (and more definitely sexuality) is not located at the upper levels of this hierarchy! It seems that gender tends to be viewed more as a concern, requiring some kind of intervention only when gender norms are transgressed or when some other obvious 'problem' arises.

These areas of interesting late-night or early-morning conversations became the focus of the interviews with our feminist scholar colleagues explored in this chapter.

Doing the research

The feminist scholars interviewed included our colleagues: Mindy Blaise and Bronwyn Davies from Australia, Veronica Pacini-Ketchabaw from Canada, and Debbie Epstein and Jen Lyttleon-Smith from the UK. The interviews covered several main areas: what each perceived as their major contributions to the understanding of gender and power in the field of early childhood; what they perceived to be the main theoretical shifts in gender and power; their critical perspectives on current understandings of gender and power dominating the early childhood education field; what they considered to be the relationship between feminist post-structuralism (FPS) and feminist new-materialism (FNM)/feminist post-humanism (FPH); what they viewed to be the generative potential of post-humanist methodologies in understanding ethics, gender and power; the approaches they engaged in to demonstrate the relevance and usefulness of post-humanist methodologies around gender, ethics and power to early childhood educators; what they viewed to be the major issues related to gender in contemporary times relevant to early childhood education; and their perspectives on whether gender is still considered central to early childhood educators' work with children or if it has indeed fallen off the educational agenda.

This research project was totally dependent on the engagement of human, non-human and more-than-human subjects in its production, intra-acting across time, space and different geopolitical contexts – a process of 'spacetimemattering' (Barad, 2007). Conducting the interviews largely involved the use of technology (mobile phones and computers, which ever worked best at the time with unstable internet access!) and utilizing Zoom or Skype to bridge different geolocations and time zones (Australia, Canada and England – often one beginning the day and the other ending it – sometimes both in pyjamas!). In contrast, some interviews were done in person, at the kitchen table, sharing food snacks and tea! This relationship with technology continued throughout the project as we relistened to interview audio files and reviewed interview transcripts (shared in Dropbox), inserting ourselves into the margins of the interview transcripts, highlighting points of interest and identifying and analysing emerging discourses (in the Foucaultian sense).

Eve Tuck and Rachel McKenzie (2015a: 19) remind us that 'we cannot escape mental processes of thought and language', which are important aspects of researching social life. Analysing how discourse is taken up and embodied by subjects, its impact on everyday practices and relations of power, and how it underpins micro- and macro-politics is critical in social science research. In terms of exploring gender in early childhood, Bronwyn Davies's early feminist post-structural research, epitomized in *Frogs and Snails and Feminist Tales* (1989) and *Shards of Glass* (1993), demonstrated the power of binary gender discourses in young children's lives and the difficulty of creating new narratives. Davies identified the constitutive force of language, how desire is shaped, and how male and female become embodied. The interviews, as linguistic accounts of life, provide a critical means through which to examine the scholars' engagements and identifications with discourse; what taken-for-granted knowledge or 'truths' are constituted within the discourses; to identify counter discourses; and to ascertain, if possible, the impact of discourse on individual practices. A discourse analysis, as a linguistic approach, provides an understanding of the relationship between language, knowledge, ideology and power (Lupton, 1992). Deborah Lupton, states:

> Discourse analysis is composed of two main dimensions: the textual and contextual. Textual dimensions are those that account for the *structures* of discourses, while contextual dimensions relate these structural descriptions of various properties to the *social, political or cultural context* in which they take place. (1992: 145)

Demonstrating what Barad calls a 're-turn', Lupton in more recent times has looked to the multilayering material-discursive potential of new materialist/post-humanist perspectives to provide an additional way of thinking about how humans live with digital technologies (Pink et al., 2017). This research into humans living with digital technologies has seen a re-turning to the significance of situated knowledge to account for the digital materiality of everyday environments. Lupton's engagement with new materialist perspectives was seen as a means to articulating the dynamic intra-actions between humans, the more-than-human and contemporary environments we live in and move through.

Within a post-structuralist framework, discourses are historically and culturally formulated modes through which we understand knowledge, power and subjectivity. According to Foucault (1974: 49), discursive practices systematically produce the subjects and objects of knowledge practices. Discourses are about who can speak, in what contexts and with what authority. Barad (2008: 137), somewhat echoing Foucaultian perspective, argues that 'to think of discourse as mere spoken or written words forming descriptive statements is to enact the mistake of representationalist thinking. Discourse is not what is said; it is that which constrains and enables what can be said. Discursive practices define what counts as meaningful statements'. 'Statements and subjects emerge from a field of possibilities,' Barad (2008: 137) goes on to point out, and 'this field of possibilities is not static or singular, but rather, it is dynamic and contingent multiplicity'.

Listening to children as doers and knowers of gender

One of the core discourses identified by the scholars is the child as agentic subject who is a doer and knower of gender. Within this perspective, children are not only viewed to be aware subjects who negotiate, mobilize and invest in gender discourses they have access to in their everyday lives but are also considered agentic subjects who are actively involved in reconceptualizing gender through gender performance (Butler, 1990). Children as knowers and doers of gender is reinforced through discourse of post-developmentalism, which challenges positivist theories of child development. Post-developmentalism contests the taken-for-granted construction of the 'normal' child founded upon universal, biologically determined linear chronological stages of development at specific ages, as exemplified in Piagetian child development theory. Within this understanding of child development and of the 'normal' child, the diversity and sociocultural and economic differences, on both micro and macro levels, across children's lives, are eclipsed. The sociocultural and geographical environments in which children's daily lives are practised and enacted, including their interactions with others – human and non-human – are central to their experiences, learning (acquisition of cultural knowledge) and development (Wulf, 2011). Mindy Blaise in her interview points out that traditional Piagetian developmentalism is foundational to the hyper-separation of the child from the material world and distracts or takes the focus away from the everyday politics of gender, as well as race, class and sexuality, including the intersections or entanglements of these with gender and each other. Positivist developmentalist perspectives of childhood undermine children's agency in the world, their critical thinking and their contributions to knowledge production, largely constituting them as passive and innocent (Robinson, 2013), through the reinforcement of binary relations of knowledge and power – for example, adult–child, male–female and white–black binaries.

Debbie Epstein, a pioneering leader in the field of sexuality in schooling since the early 1990s, made the important acknowledgement, when interviewed, that children have something to tell us about gender if we listen. Bronwyn Davies's (2014) recent work in *Listening to Children* takes up the concept of 'listening' and also highlights the importance of listening to children, stating: 'In order to listen to children in a way that respects and enables the contribution to their communities that they might make, one must be open to being affected.' Davies elaborates on these ideas further, commenting:

> Listening is about being open to being affected. It is about being open to difference and, in particular, to difference in all its multiplicity as it emerges in each moment in between oneself and another. Listening is about *not* being bound by what you already know. It is life a movement. Listening to children is not just a matter of good pedagogy; encounters with others, where each is open to being affected by the other, is integral, I suggest, to life itself.

Veronica Pacini-Ketchabaw, Mindy Blaise and Jen Lyttleton-Smith, working from FNM/FPH perspectives point out that it is not just about *listening* to what children say but also about observing what they are doing and how they are creating new worlds. Engaging with Baradian understandings to explore 'community' and 'ethics', Davies (2014) argues:

> Children open themselves up in multiple ways to new possibilities, and in doing so make the very basis of an ethical community possible. Participation in an ethical community serves to enhance the specificity of each child, and at the same time, to enhance each child's capacity to actively participate in the making of community in all its emergent multiplicity. Communities, then, are emergent mattering, engaged, in Barad's terms, in bringing forth new worlds, engaged in reconfiguring the world.

Increasingly, children and young people are challenging through both language and the doing of gender, the discourse of a normative stable, binary gender (male/female), and the discourse that there are only two possible genders linked to one's sexed body. Young people are choosing to identify across a range of gender categories that they are naming and practising to describe and express their gendered selves. Some identify as gender fluid, gender queer, gender diverse, non-binary, androgynous, agender, gender non-conforming, bi-gender, transgender, sistergirls and brotherboys, to name just a few (Robinson et al., 2014). The social network medium Facebook, in recognition of this shift in young people's perspectives and practices around gender identity and expression, provides over seventy different gender options for UK users and fifty for US users to choose from when signing up to this platform. The acknowledgement of multiple gender categories is not a new material-discursive phenomenon. Prior to European Christian settlement in some countries (e.g. the United States and Australia), indigenous communities recognized more than two genders.

For example, Native American communities recognized five gender categories: female, male, two spirit female, two spirit male and transgender (Davis, 2016). The resistance to acknowledging, accepting and respecting multiple gender categories and gender fluidity continues today.

Debbie Epstein pointed out that some early childhood educators have an investment in reinforcing gender binaries, potentially out of fear on the part of educators, of making children targets of discrimination and bullying. However, it is also likely linked to normative understandings of gender and of childhood inherent in hegemonic discourses of developmentalism. The investments that early childhood educators generally have in the discourses of developmentalism and childhood innocence were acknowledged by Mindy Blaise, who argued that the discourse of childhood innocence is 'holding the early childhood field back' – on many different levels. The childhood innocence discourse is reinforced by developmentalism, which essentializes childhood innocence as an inherent aspect of Western childhood – particularly of the white, middle-class, female child. This discourse and its impact on understandings of childhood and practices with children have been the focus of considerable research in recent years (see Jackson, 1982; Kitzinger, 1990; Corteen & Scraton, 1997; Gittins, 1998; Bruhm & Hurley, 2004; Renold, 2005; Taylor, 2007; Bhana, 2008; Blaise, 2009, 2010; Egan & Hawkes, 2010; Robinson, 2008, 2012, 2013). Children's normative behaviours are highly regulated and policed, officially and informally, in their everyday lives by adults and other children (Robinson, 2013). Epstein's research with nursery-aged children in the UK in the mid-1990s pointed out that gender binaries, gender stereotypes and heteronormativity are central to the institution of schooling. Epstein (1995: 57) comments:

> School is an important locus for the inscription of gender and of heterosexuality and that it is, therefore, also an important locus for challenging dominant discourses of (hetero)sexism.

Schools are a core site in the constitution of young people's sexual and gender subjectivities. Jen Gilbert (2014: xiv) has argued: 'Sexuality saturates educational spaces, objects and relations.' Research in primary schools highlights how curricula, teacher practices and children's peer cultures constitute, reinforce and perpetuate heteronormative discourses of gender and sexuality (Allen & Ingram, 2015; Fields, 2008; Fields & Payne, 2016; Gilbert, 2014; Maria Kromidas; Renold, 2005; Robinson, 2013; Robinson & Davies, 2008; Thorne, 1993).

Research conducted by Robinson and Jones Diaz (2000, 2006) with Australian early childhood educators in the early 2000s also demonstrated that gender binary practices, gender stereotypes and heteronormativity were strong among participants in the study. This point was further reinforced in research conducted with early childhood educators in Western Australia and the Northern Territory in 2012 (Davies & Robinson, 2012). Research undertaken in London, around the same time (Osgood, 2012), found much the same situation among early childhood educators, where childhood innocence discourses and the promotion of heteronormative practices prevailed. Current practices in Australia in some early childhood settings suggest that there have been minimal changes in practices in this country in terms of addressing gender binaries, heteronormativity and gender equity in children's early education over the past two decades. Encouraging and hosting whole setting approaches to children's mock weddings exemplifies some of the approaches to gender that still prevail in some contexts. These large-scale heteronormative mock weddings involve children dressing up in bride and groom clothing, sending out invitations to families, encouraging parents to bring along wedding photos, conducting a mock marriage ceremony and a wedding celebration feast. Children's uncritical participation in such gendered events limits their perceived options in life, regardless of their cultural backgrounds, and conveys strict gendered expectations of young girls' and boys' futures. The dismissal of, or the refusal to engage in, similar elaborate events depicting the mock weddings of two boys or two girls who wish to marry each other reflects the way that early childhood education perpetuates (hetero)gender and sexuality norms. The impact of marriage equality (same-sex marriage) laws in the UK, Europe, the United States and, more recently, Australia on early childhood education policies and practices awaits to be seen.

Childhood is a critical period in which children are interpellated as 'good' citizen subjects, which is discursively constituted in white, middle-class, heteronormative, Christian morals and values (Bell & Binnie, 2000; Berlant, 1997; Richardson, 1998; Robinson, 2013). Childhood innocence is an essential commodity in this process, as well as in maintaining adult–child binary relationships of power in which children's agency is curbed and their vulnerabilities to abuses of power are increased. Innocence is generally vehemently defended in Western society as an inherent and definitive component of normative childhood. Ironically, the apolitical child is utilized to reproduce and regulate (heterogendered) normative subjectivity, reflected in government laws and policies, as well as in media and popular culture (Berlant, 1997; Bruhm & Hurley, 2004; Kincaid, 2004). Alternative imaginings of childhood (and adulthood) and of children's gender subjectivities are generally rendered problematic as reflected through the resistance demonstrated by some adults and children to different ways of doing gender. Moral panic often prevails when normative values, especially heteronormative values, are transgressed (Berlant, 2004; Kincaid, 2004; Robinson, 2008; Robinson & Davies, 2010; Taylor, 2007).

Discourses of developmentalism and innocence work to both constitute and regulate early childhood education environments as apolitical spaces, a point reiterated by the feminist scholars we interviewed. Early childhood educators generally view politics as not relevant to children or to their early learning (Robinson & Jones Diaz, 2006). Both discourses effectively distract from the political, in particular the politics of gender, sexuality, social class, ethnicity and ability (and so on), which are foundational to children's everyday experiences. Blaise identified domestic violence as one of the critical issues confronting Australian women, pointing out that early childhood education should be playing a core role in challenging the gender and power foundations of violence against women and girls. Gender stereotypes in early childhood contribute to the perpetuation of certain discourses about gender and power that underpin domestic violence and sexual violence against women and girls, and the violence experienced by some men who do not fit hegemonic discourses of masculinity. Disrupting the discourses and practices that lead to this violence, including the maldistribution of social and economic resources across the genders, is critical. Equally, providing more equitable and alternative counter-narratives of gender and power is essential and foundational to early childhood education programmes aimed at building respectful and ethical relationships early in life in terms of gender and sexuality.

When asked if gender has been taken off the early childhood agenda, Bronwyn Davies commented that early childhood educators are often

> locked into a moral order (Deleuze), where they don't have to think, where they are in a constant line of descent. The possibility of something new is not there … The capacity to be thinking, alive subjects engaged in lines of flight with children, or with the researcher who comes to work with them, are taken away by packages.

The packages that Davies refers to in this comment are resources or pedagogical tool kits on which many educators rely. Within the neo-liberal framework of many early childhood education classrooms, gender, like other aspects of diversity and difference (e.g. class, race, sexuality, ethnicity and so on), is not on the agenda. Davies's work in Scandinavian schools indicates that gender goes on and off the early childhood education agenda; it becomes a focus when it is perceived as necessary, when an issue arises, bringing it to the attention of educators. As in most early childhood education environments, educators may often need to be made aware of gender issues and inequities by 'outsiders' (researchers, scholars, activists, trainee teachers, some parents). However, Davies points out that experimentation, creativity and openness to new ways of thinking and doing are stifled by bureaucratic processes, controls and regulations required in neo-liberal contexts.

Challenging human exceptionalism: Entanglements with the material world

A core discourse of the child in feminist new materialism/feminist post-humanism is the child as entangled within the material world – the child is not a separate entity but formed from and with its material environment and with the non-human. According to Veronica Pacini-Ketchabaw, the focus within this theoretical perspective shifts from critique, language and deconstruction as in feminist post-structuralism, to a focus on children's practices, doings and world-making – the creation of new and different worlds (as pointed out above by Bronwyn Davies). There is recognition that the world is in constant movement and individuals, including children, have the agency to create different worlds. This raises critical questions about what type of worlds we want children to make and what ethical questions we want children to think about when creating new worlds, argues Veronica Pacini-Ketchabaw. It is questions such as these that have been foundational to Blaise's and Pacini-Ketchabaw's involvement in the development of the Common Worlds Research Collective, an international interdisciplinary network of researchers whose focus is on relations with the more-than-human world (http://commonworlds.net). Within this context, researchers from early childhood education, childhood studies, children's and more-than-human geographies, environmental education, FNM, and indigenous and environmental humanities address issues of ethical and sustainable relationships between human societies and natural environments. Based on Latour's (2004) notion of 'common worlds', the network focuses on 'the ways in which our past, present and future lives are entangled with those of other beings, non-living entities, technologies, elements, discourses, forces, landforms'. One core strand of research involves inquiries into children's common world relations with place, with the material world and with other species.

Blaise, mobilizing the works of theorists, such as Donna Haraway, Deborah Bird Rose, Thom Van Doreen and Val Plumwood, challenges the discourse of human exceptionalism. Blaise argues that teachers are not separate entities from children, but rather teachers and children are integrally intertwined and entangled with the material world in which they live. Within FNM/FPH, teaching and learning are complicated and politicized through a shift away from the discourse of 'professional knowing' of children to a space where body and mind are not separated as in more traditional liberal humanist binary understandings of the human and the world. Blaise comments:

> It is moving from always knowing the child and knowing the child from a professional distance; instead teaching new teachers and practising teachers that they, and their teaching gendered bodies are not separate from child bodies and more-than-human bodies, and this could be the materials they are working with like paper, clay, paint, or the bodies of animals and plants.

As a consequence of this shift, early childhood teaching becomes no longer just about children, but rather it is about 'paying attention in radically different ways', Blaise argues, to children's relational entanglements with the more-than-human – trees, the wind, dogs and so on.

What happens to politics in new materialism/post-humanism?

A common critique of new materialism/post-humanism has been its potentiality to easily lose a critical 'political edge'. Epstein, mobilizing a humanist materialist approach to educational research on sexuality, gender, race and class in school contexts over many decades, has aimed to address the question: 'How do the privileged remain in place?'. Epstein critiques the shift to new materialism, arguing that its micro focus on *matter* has the potential to trivialize or obscure larger concerns of inequality (e.g. sexism, racism, homophobia, transphobia), potentially 'losing site of the sedimentary layering of power in society'. Epstein maintains, ethnography, a methodological approach examining the minutiae in the 'moment' and within 'context', central to her own research, is critical to an analysis of broader sociocultural relations of power. Epstein argues that a materialist approach, which keeps history, the social and the cultural in context, is necessary for addressing broad social inequalities. The new materialist agenda, which is not concerned with representation or context, she surmises, has the potential to feed into the neo-liberal agenda of individualism. Epstein concludes by questioning whether the shift to new materialism is a 'progressive or a reactionary move' – of 'following the fashion'.

The new-materialist/post-humanist scholars interviewed were aware of the possibilities within the theoretical frameworks of new materialism/ post-humanism of losing a critical political lens, particularly in terms of the inequalities highlighted by Epstein. Veronica Pacini-Ketchabaw commented that new materialists/post-humanists 'need to think a bit deeper to bring in the political'. Pacini-Ketchabaw acknowledged the critical 'political edge' feminist perspectives bring to new materialism/post-humanism. However, Pacini-Ketchabaw argues there is a point where being caught in a focus on 'critique' can become problematic, stifling ways forward, commenting, 'political work can easily be lost if we don't have that critique but at the same time we cannot just critique'. Pacini-Ketchabaw highlights the work of Donna Haraway to exemplify how it is possible for new materialists to maintain a political edge, engaging with feminist perspectives, without getting caught up in the need to constantly go back to the critique.

The relationship of feminism to FPS and FPH was discussed in the interviews. It was generally agreed that feminism is central to giving a critical, political and ethical focus to both post-humanism and post-structuralism. Feminist theory provides a perspective and method to reconfigure what it means to be human, and it has always been critical of the ways in which masculinist discourse has underpinned positivist modernist views of the 'human' and how masculine ways of knowing have been privileged, especially in the sciences (Haraway, 1988). Providing a critique of the privileging of white, middle-class, continental, male theorists, these feminist scholars spoke about the importance of bringing back a feminist perspective to the discussions of the material and discursive subjectivity, performativity and change. Veronica Pacini-Ketchabaw commented: *There is always something that takes me back to feminist perspectives.* Feminism has always had at its core a perspective and method that has been about reconceptualizing and reconfiguring the human and what it means to be human. Historically, modernist discourses, foundational to the sciences, portrayed the human within a white masculine framework. Donna Haraway's earlier work focused on challenging the masculine bias in scientific culture. Veronica Pacini-Ketchabaw concluded:

> I do not have a lot of problems in terms of bringing in the new materialist perspective but I think it needs to be done in a way that starts from acknowledging that bringing in new materialism is not because the critique was

bad or unnecessary but only because it has been appropriated by capitalism and neo-liberalism, so what do we need to do now?

In re-turning to Haraway's (1988) situated knowledge, there is a refocusing on the partiality of knowledge and the importance of standpoint (situated in relations of multiplicity) and positioning. Haraway (1988: 580) states: 'We need the power of modern critical theories of how meanings and bodies get made, not in order to deny meanings and bodies but in order to build meanings and bodies that have a chance for life.'

What is the relationship between feminist post-structuralism and feminist post-humanism?

A focus of this book has been to explore the relationship between FPS and FNM/ FPH. We have argued throughout the book that it can be viewed as a relationship of mutual benefit – one in which each builds on the other, bringing different but equally important perspectives, in this case, to an understanding of gender (and sexuality subjectivity). Echoing Barad, Bronwyn Davies argues that the work done by FPH is not a radical break away from FPS but rather is an extension of it Davies (2018). In our interview with Davies, she commented: *I think what new materialism has done particularly from Barad, but also from Deleuze, and people like Bergson, is made it possible for a whole lot of the things that were happening, and have been happening in post-structuralist theory, to be taken a step further.* Davies considers the theoretical shift has been one that has moved from a focus on reflexive methodology of getting children to see how they embody and do gender and the constitutive impact of discourse to a diffractive approach. Diffraction, according to Haraway (1992: 300), is a metaphor for rethinking relationality (difference) through identifying 'interference', which is different to replication, reflection or reproduction. Haraway says: 'A diffraction pattern does not map where differences appear, but rather maps where the effects of differences appear'. Davies sees this shift being foreshadowed by Deleuze and Guattari's assemblages and Bergson's lines of descent (endless clichéd repetitions of the world which hold the world in place) and ascent (what disrupts that and enables something new to emerge). Davies argues that Karen Barad, whose work has been foundational for post-humanist scholars, has introduced an emphasis on matter to feminist post-structuralism – that is, the way that matter is made to matter. Barad argues that post-structuralist approaches have not taken account of 'non-human' agency. Matter in feminist post-structuralism, according to

Davies, echoing Barad, has focused on human matter at the expense of non-human matter – a framework in which humans are given ascendency. Exploring entanglements, she points out, leads to the possibility of further deconstruction.

Our interviews with FNM/FPH scholars generally highlighted an uneasiness with the focus in feminist post-structuralism on critique, deconstruction and problematizing, with some expressing frustration about this leading to paralysis, a sense of despair and futility about how change is possible within this framework. Still, the 'messiness' of FPH was commented on by Veronica Pacini-Ketchabaw. Mindy Blaise's shift to FPH has been about becoming 'unstuck' and refocusing attention on the ontological and ethical. However, Davies points out: *To actually bring about lasting change is an extraordinarily complex thing to do because of this tendency for it to go back into the already known, and because of the way the new actually depends on, is inter-woven with, the already known.* As we have pointed out, this shift to the 'new' is not so new but owes considerable indebtedness to indigenous knowledge systems; other feminist theorists, including FPS; post-colonialists; and queer theorists who have pathed the way, opening up different material-discursive ways of seeing and being in the world.

As discussed in the introductory chapter of this book, Karen Barad challenges the reading of her work as a moving away from the critical work of feminist post-structuralism. For Barad, continuity is crucial, arguing that the writings of feminist post-structuralists, such as Butler, cannot be overlooked or forgotten but rather are foundational to new and different readings that extend this work. Some of the feminist scholars whom we interviewed reflected on the generosity often extended by feminist theorists like Barad to other theorists who have gone before and how this contrasted with the approach of men scholars working with post-humanism.

Mindy Blaise's shift to FNM was primarily about incorporating collaborative, multisensory, multi-species and affective ethnography as the basis of her work – that is, being 'out and about', as Blaise put it. Within this theoretical framework, the focus is on ethico-political practice, and Blaise identifies several theorists whose research has been influential to her own – Donna Haraway's focus on acting in the moment, response-ability and awareness of vulnerability; Thom Van Dooren's work in environmental humanities; Val Plumwood's ecofeminist philosophy; and the works of Indigenous scholars such as Deborah Bird Rose. These theorists bring affect, reconstructing new relationships, seeing and doing things differently, and ethics to the fore of their work. However, Blaise does point out that these concepts are 'not beyond the scope of feminist poststructuralism', which focuses on power, discourse/knowledge, deconstructing binaries, differences, the politics manifested in different contexts and pinpointing the ethical/unethical. Blaise comments: *Feminist new materialism ... it has given me a way to write about and do my research in more political ways. Or to push my work further I guess and it is just not about talk and thinking about ideas, it is about the doings, happenings, and how I am entangled with it as well.*

FNM's/FPH's concerns with intra-active, entanglements between human, non-human, the more-than-human and the utilization of a diffractive lens result in becoming attuned to the unpredictable possibilities that these relations and ways of seeing might open up other ways to be in, engage with and produce different worlds (Haraway's worldling/and worldliness). Reconstruction rather than deconstruction is at the fore. Blaise spoke about the importance of affect as a possible means through which change is produced and enacted, pointing out that affective pedagogy is a useful approach especially in relation to working in the areas of diversity and difference and social justice, which is about teaching for discursive and material change at both the individual and institutional levels (micro and macro).

Jennifer Lyttleton-Smith also argues that feminist post-humanism is not opposed to FPS and that both are about embracing diversity, complexity and power. FPS is more about patterns of reference, she points out, and how everyday relations play out – how identity is played out in regard to race, class, sexuality, etc., and individuals' capacity for agency in relation to identity. FPH, on the other hand, she comments, is about micro relations. Within this framework, it is much more possible to lose sight of the macro relations, that is, the broader patterns of oppression, suppression, dominance and submission, and how race, gender, class and sexuality are produced. Grand narratives, Lyttleton-smith maintains, produce constructions to 'fall into', but FPH is about analysing the negotiation of power between subjects and objects and temporality on a daily basis – a perspective that is often lost in social narratives of discrimination. Essentializing notions of tolerance and acceptance denies everyday experiences, and FPH can offer tracking of micro-moments through intersectionality of subjectivity.

Lyttleton-Smith, within a Baradian framework, argues for a collaborative relationship between FPS and FPH, a position in which discourse and materiality work together and broader relations of power are kept in focus. This approach is reflected in her doctoral research with nursery school children. Lyttleton-Smith incorporated a Baradian theoretical analysis to explore how children's gendered subjectivities are produced. Starting the project with Butlerian and Foucaultian perspectives to examine gender, discourse and power, Lyttleton-Smith shifted to a different perspective to more effectively articulate the relationship, observed over the time of the project, between the materiality of the nursery engaging in tandem with children's social and physical changes, as well as her situated entanglements within the minute enfoldings within the research encounters she reported on (Lyttleton-Smith, 2017). Lyttleton-Smith found utilizing discursive analysis with younger children frustrating as they were often silent, did not hold conversations that were linear, but were chaotic, disjointed and temporal. This point is widely recognized in the field of early childhood education, which has led to the development and widespread usage of more creative methodologies such as drawing, ethnographic observations or photography and using images/stories to initiate discussions. Lyttleton-Smith shifted her focus to observing children's bodies and entanglements with material things and their interactions with other children and the environment, which ultimately proved more productive.

Gender matters!

The current focus on shifting and multiple performances of gender, as identified in the beginning of this chapter, has opened up discussions on gender fluidity within feminist academia/childhood studies but has equally shut down conversations as a result of a conservative backlash from government, media, conservative politicians and community members to these ideas. Foucault's (1980) power/discourse and governmentality offer critical frameworks in which to understand how in these instances the state exercises power to govern broad populations. In recent times, backlash around gender fluidity and non-binary gender has resulted in government interventions into measures of inclusion for gender diverse and transgender young people in schools, not just through controlling what is in the curricula but also through controlling the materiality of school spaces such as the lack of gender-neutral toilets. This state intervention is often a result of pressure from powerful media outlets, influenced by conservative politicians and members of the community, that perpetuate particular claims of 'truth' about non-binary gender and fluidity as a form of 'political correctness' gone 'too far'. One of the first actions of the Trump administration in the United States was to revoke federal protections, installed by the Obama administration, for transgender students that instructed schools to allow them to use the bathrooms and locker rooms matching their gender identities (https://www.telegraph.co.uk/news/2017/02/23/donald-trump-revokes-barack-obama-guidelines-transgender-bathrooms/).

Veronica Pacini-Ketchabaw argues that there is a need to engage with different thinking around the role of biology, gendered bodies and materialism in relation to gender subjectivity. Lyttleton-Smith is critical of the biological and discursive essentialism that can prevail around understandings of the development of gender subjectivity. Biology and discourse do not 'make' children do gender, but rather children can inhabit multiple gender subjectivities, are fluid and dynamic, and are not fixed in discourse or biology. Gender is produced in different ways through social and material contexts. As Simone de Beauvior proclaimed in *The Second Sex* (1949), 'One is not born, but rather becomes, a woman.' For Lyttleton-Smith, gender is produced through discourse and bodies in material-discursive entanglements within spatial temporal contexts – that is 'spacetimemattering'. Utilizing a Baradian post-humanist perspective of performativity (iterative intra-activity), Lyttleton-Smith views gender as becoming within each event, entanglement and moment, opening up possibilities for reconfiguring gender differently in the next moment. Barad (2003: 826) argues:

> Posthumanist formulations of performativity makes evident the importance of taking account of 'human', 'nonhuman', and 'cyborgian' forms of agency (indeed all such material-discursive forms). This is both possible and necessary because agency is a matter of changes in the apparatuses of bodily production, and such changes take place through various intra-actions, some of which remake the boundaries that delineate differential constitutions of the 'human'.

Barad's perspective is different from that of Butler's iterative citationality performativity. In Butler's theorization of performativity, gender requires a performance that is repeated, but these repetitions do not always produce stability of meaning. Each repetition is done in different contexts, circumstances and times, producing different meanings, rendering it indeterminate and sometimes unpredictable, as Butler (1993: 226) comments: 'Let us remember that reiterations are never simply replicas of the same'. Butler (1990: 145) does not see regulatory norms of discourses as fully determining, pointing out: 'If the rules governing signification not only restrict, but enable the assertion of alternative domains of cultural possibility, i.e. new possibilities for gender, that contest the rigid codes of hierarchical binarisms, then it is only within practices of repetitive signifying that a subversion of identity becomes possible.'

Conclusion: #Gender still matters

Gender continues to matter in the context of recognizing and addressing the inequities associated with the micro and macro relations of power associated with gender. The recent #MeToo social media phenomenon brought attention to the widespread prevalence of sexual assault and harassment that have plagued women's personal and professional lives by men who have exploited women in their positions of authority and power. The material-discursive readings of this phenomenon highlight the importance of acknowledging the politics of gender and its sociocultural and economic impacts, as well as the ways in which this phenomenon is embodied in women's everyday lives.

For some women, academia continues to be a space in which these practices and others are too often part of the educational and workplace experience. #FEAS (Feminist Educators Against Sexism) is also a contemporary acknowledgement of sexism in the academy and other educational spaces. Like this project, it too emerged out of the conversations between feminist scholars and the need to address the ways in which women's voices, theory and philosophy were marginalized. A commitment to illuminating sexist practices and their intersections across other areas of oppression, within and beyond the broader structures of the university, are core to the group's brief.

Decades of educational research, particularly by feminist scholars, have demonstrated that much of the inequitable gendered discourses and practices that prevail are embedded in children's early lives. A question that arose in the interviews was around the role of early childhood educators in addressing these early foundations of material-discursive practices around gender inequality. Is there enough time or space to address gender in the daily pedagogies of early childhood education? The perceived lack of time and relevance has tended to underpin the resistances to doing this work with children. There is no denying that early childhood education environments are extremely busy spaces, especially with broader professional pressures, impacting on daily practices. However, 'doing' gender work with children should not be a burdensome add-on to the daily programme but, like diversity and social justice work more generally, needs to be integral to everyday material and discursive practices and pedagogical moments. Since children are routinely playing with gender in early childhood, it would not require a seismic leap from early childhood educators to engage with the world-making practices that are unfolding in everyday play and in the in-between spaces in early childhood contexts (see Lyttleton-Smith, 2015; Osgood, 2014, 2018). The following chapters in this volume provide lively illustrations of how we – adults, feminist researchers –are able to extend our ideas about gender by deeply immersing ourselves in the 'what if' questions about gender (as produced through processes and micro-moments) in early childhood.

4

'I Like Your Costume': Dress-up Play and Feminist Trans-theoretical Shifts

Jen Lyttleton-Smith and Kerry H. Robinson

Introduction

In this chapter we discuss different theoretical approaches to analysing and interpreting the ways in which young children dress up their bodies in gendering and queering ways, namely feminist post-structuralist (FPS), queer theory and post-humanist (PH). In doing so, we discuss the advantages, intersections, difficulties and tensions associated with these different theoretical frameworks. In terms of situating ourselves theoretically, we each have come from, and currently come to this discussion with, sometimes differing, intersecting and shifting/emerging perspectives in terms of our relationships with these theories, but our perspectives do align at certain critical points. Historically, Kerry Robinson comes from a feminist theoretical background, taking up feminist post-structuralist and queer theory approaches in her work on childhood, gender and sexuality in order to address the difficulties associated with earlier feminist frameworks. Jen Lyttleton-Smith began her career embedded in feminist post-structuralism but has later developed an appreciation for the materially located insight offered by post-humanist concepts, applying them in her work within a multilayered approach. For both of us, theoretically analysing gender in childhood to understand how we become gendered subjects and how gender, power and inequality intersect is core to our work. We consider post-humanism to be most effectively used not as a replacement for analyses of power and discourse but as an additional layer of analysis that enhances post-structural perspectives.

This chapter explores a reciprocal relationship between our research interpretations of gender performativity and children's clothing and our understandings of our theoretical performativity as feminist scholars of gender and childhood. There is a sense, then, that this chapter covers two distinct topics, each of which enhances understandings of the other; the first is how in adopting temporal transgressive forms of dress the child body is opened up to new and, sometimes, queer or otherwise transgressive ways of experiencing gender and sexuality. Through a series of brief data extracts from each of our fieldwork encounters with children and young people, we think about 'dress' and 'dress-up' as potentially transformative to expressions of gender, political and theoretical subjectivities. We explore children's negotiation of different gendered subject positions through dress, children's transgressions from gender norms in this process, children's readings of embodied gender and the ways in which gender norms are regulated in childhood. We argue that the dualistic discursive distinction between gendered 'dressing' and 'dressing-up' acts to obscure a simultaneous multiplicity of gender subjectivity where these socially weighted terms flatten to produce the self and the other as one and the same. Equally, we argue that for feminist research, post-humanism is not and need not be the 'paradigm shift' it threatens to emerge as – rendering feminist post-structuralism as outdated or irrelevant – and instead we suggest methods of layering theoretical approaches to expose the simultaneous multiplicity of research subjectivities and the interpretative nature of the data that we draw from them.

Robinson's research highlights the discursive and affective impact of dress on children, including those who identify as transgender. For one boy, transgressing gender norms through dress was an emotional process of soothing the self. However, the power of gendered discourse often eclipsed the young boy's personal experience, resulting in his questioning the gender identity of others who transgressed gender norms, in this case, an early childhood educator:

> The next day he came back, and he said to me, 'You know how you are a girl?' and I said yes. 'And I thought you were a boy'. I said yes; he said, 'Do other big people ever think you are a boy?'

In Lyttleton-Smith's research, a young boy comments on her change of clothing style, referring to her unusual dress attire as a 'costume':

> Today I am wearing a skirt which is unusual for me as I normally dress in practical trousers for nursery. Several children comment on it, saying that they like it or that I look pretty. However, the most interesting comment comes from Adam. He is sitting on the carpet and I am standing nearby. 'Jennie', he says,

slowly. 'Yes Adam?' With great sincerity, he replies, 'I like your costume.' I laugh despite myself and say, 'Thank you, Adam, that's very kind of you.'

Both comments highlight the confusion caused when others adopt aspects of dress that do not map onto what they think is representative of who you *really* are – in this instance, one's gender or position (i.e. job or role in an organization). Children negotiate and interpret the discourses available to them that constitute particular subjectivities, for example, of what a normative woman or girl or researcher or social scientist should be like and how they should behave. Dress is a powerful means through which the intelligibility of a gendered subject is established, but it is equally a powerful means through which resistances to and transgressions from binary gender norms are performed. The binary gender system, 'man'/'woman', fails to address the layering and multiplicity of gender performances and the ways in which masculinity and femininity are produced and sustained across all bodies.

The second area addressed in the chapter is how exploring new and, some say, 'fashionable' theoretical approaches opens us up as theoretically orientated researchers to different experiences of gender phenomena in childhood studies but also different discomforts and doubts around the ethics and value of what we do. The key discomfort that arises when centralizing the material is the potential to lose sight of the complex layers of socio-discursive analysis and interpretation that has so greatly benefited the feminist academic and political cause. Of particular significance here are the difficulties faced by some prominent feminist theorists in aligning post-human approaches with the recognition and exploration of intersectional power dynamics that underlie lived experiences of racism, ableism, classism and other discriminatory channels where the historical and contemporary discourse 'comes to matter' for particular bodies in particularly harmful ways (Ahmed, 2008).

Of lesser importance, but still significant, is the discomfort of how to locate oneself as a feminist researcher when post-humanism has emerged as a transformational paradigm, in the style of phenomenology, that pertains a politicized label to those who repeatedly engage with it. Its distinctive and extensive lexicon has reached such complexity that a directed encyclopaedia of its terms and their multitudinous, shifting use seem an increasingly necessary endeavour. In a politicized field of research, the recognition of and alignment with other scholars whose priorities complement one's own is of social and collaborative importance. The potential for widespread divergence within feminist sociology, where scholars are divided neatly (and, often, imprecisely) into 'post-structuralist' and 'post-humanist', presents a challenge, particularly where a sense of suspicion or cynicism – arguably exacerbated by that complex lexicon – imbues some of the more radical aspects of post-humanism.

'Dressed', 'dressed-up', 'being dressed up': Discourse, power and the politics of clothing

In this section, we set out a feminist post-structuralist (FPS) approach to children, gender and dress. It is an approach with which we feel very much aligned, while also holding an active interest in, and openness to, the alternative analytic approach offered by feminist post-humanism (FPH). FPS has provided a critical lens through which to understand the process of gender subjectification in children's lives (Blaise, 2005a, 2009, 2010; Davies, 1989, 1993; MacNaughton, 2000; Osgood, 2014, 2015a; Renold, 2005; Robinson & Davies, 2008a, 2015; Taylor & Richardson, 2005; Thorne, 1993) and gender as performative (Butler, 1990). In the dynamic, cultural process of gender construction, sexed bodies are discursively and materially inscribed with masculine and feminine attributes. Cultural narratives provide multiple representations of gender, but binary gender is discursively and materially constituted as the normal and natural expression of gender in Western societies with femininity perceived to naturally align with female bodies and masculinity with male bodies.

Within FPS and queer perspectives, gender is an unstable and contested social category where meanings and representations are susceptible to change across and within different cultures over time and across bodies. In the process of gender construction, children identify and make sense of themselves as gendered subjects – that is, boys or girls – through discourses of binary gender that are historically and culturally made available to them through family, schooling, other institutions (e.g. government, religious and faith-based), peers, media and popular culture. Children embody particular discourses of gender that they invest in and represent through their gender expression; FPS perspectives point out that discourse matters to bodies, rather than just being a matter of language. Children, like adults, are agentic subjects, who negotiate, take up, resist, dispute and transform enculturating influences and normalizing discourses they encounter. However, transgressions from gender norms, whether as children or adults, can lead to ostracism and harassment from others; children play a critical role in the policing and regulation of other children's (and adults') normative gender subjectivities (Robinson, 2013). For most children, getting gender right is important (Blaise 2005a; Davies, 1993).

Feminist post-structuralist and queer perspectives are critical to understanding broad social relations of gender and power and how these relationships manifest in inequities through macro and micro everyday interactions. Foucaultian analysis of power (particularly panoptic power), which operates through discourse, has been pivotal in demonstrating the disciplinary impact of power through regulatory practices of surveillance and normalization. Subjectivities are produced in negotiation with existing relations of power/'regimes of truth', and gendered subjectivities are negotiated and regulated through normative male–female binary relations. Through the process of panoptic control (individual self-surveillance), individuals commit to a coherent performance of gender. Butler's (1990) heterosexual matrix has been crucial in demonstrating the operation of the regulation of gender. Through this 'grid of cultural intelligibility' bodies, genders and desires are naturalized; with gender intelligibility achieved through a discursive/epistemic model in which for bodies to cohere and make sense, it is assumed 'that there must be a stable sex expressed through a stable gender (masculine expresses male, feminine expresses female) that is oppositionally and hierarchically defined through the compulsory practice of heterosexuality' (Butler, 1990: 151).

Dress is integral to the perpetuation of a heteronormative binary gender, differentiating male and female bodies, and a powerful means through which the intelligibility of a gendered subject is established (McRobbie, 1994; Blaise, 2005a; Davies, 1993; Renold, 2005). It is also core to the ways in which the differentiation between multiple femininities and masculinities is established (Blaise, 2005b; Renold, 2005). Blaise's research into children's gendered subjectivities in early childhood demonstrated how children's engagement with dress/fashion was critical to performances of gender identity, the reinforcement and perpetuation of heteronormativity, and the establishment of friendship groups. Dress/fashion, as a form of social capital, often underpinned children's popularity among peers. Blaise identified discourses of gender prevalent among the young girls in her study, including 'girly-girls' and 'cool-girls,' each identified through particular dress; girly-girls represented through hyperfeminine clothing (e.g. frills, lace, dresses, skirts), and cool-girls identified by bell-bottom pants, baseball cap turned back and Spice Girl logos (the fashion of the time!). Blaise (2005a: 62) points out the differential impact of gendered clothing on the everyday experiences of girls and boys, commenting:

> Clothes enforce a different set of rules for the girls, which necessitate very clear limits on their behavior. Boys, on the other hand, are never observed worrying

about how their clothing prevents them from participating in activities or being a certain kind of boy while sitting and listening to stories on the rug.

Being girly-girls did not necessarily lead to popularity and power; they were generally restricted in engaging in active and messy activities and were often viewed by others as playing it safe in their dress. Wearing trousers and shirts was a means through which to access a more powerful feminine subject position. However, the position of power was established more so through tapping into the discourse of hegemonic masculinity. Of particular importance were the ways in which the intersections of class, gender and race work together in relation to dress/fashion to differentiate access to power among peers (Reay, 2001).

Emma Renold's (2005: 43) research with primary school children raised similar issues around gender and dress/fashion, commenting: 'Clothes were a central source of social and sexual capital and one of the most visible social and cultural markers of differentiated femininities and differentiated friendship groups.' Renold (2005) demonstrated how girly-girls, positioned in what she calls the flirty-fashion discourse, were engaging in certain discursive practices and bodily performances of gender, involving dress/fashion techniques (e.g. rolling up the waistband of school skirts, applying mascara and lip gloss). Through such practices, girls bodied were constituted as both objects and subjects of heterosexual desire. Girly-girls, Renold (2005: 44) argued, were 'flirting with sexual boundaries of asexual/sexual child and the gendered generational boundaries of adult or teenage woman/girl-child'.

The dress-up corner

Children's 'dress ups' generally reflect the ways in which children take up characters of their own gender and play out powerful desires, fantasies and real-life discourses. The 'dress-up corner' in early childhood is a space in which children are generally free to engage in taking up different personas and characters, acting out fantastical narratives, experimenting with gender and rehearsing expectations of future lives as adults. Scavenging through boxes of discarded clothes for that special outfit, children discursively and materially slip into a variety of characters, momentarily becoming princesses, firefighters, nurses, pirates, mothers, fathers, brides and many more. However, the 'dress up corner' and dressing up more generally is a gendered time and space. This play is highly influenced by discourses in children's popular culture of the time but is also representative and constitutive of gendered relations of power more broadly – it is a political space in which heteronormative binary gender discourses regulate children's dressing up.

Children's mock weddings, for example, have become highly produced extravaganzas in some early childhood settings (in Australia), involving not just children and early childhood educators but also parents, siblings and extended family members. In these pretend wedding ceremonies, children act out the marriage ritual in wedding attire in front of peers and families; parents are encouraged to bring their own wedding photos and other marriage memorabilia, and cake, representative of wedding cake, is served at the end of the ceremony in a carnivalesque atmosphere. These events, initiated and encouraged by some educators and families, tap into children's enjoyment and excitement for dressing up, as well as their desires and enthusiasm to enact marriage ceremonies in their play. As Robinson and Davies (2015: 180) argue the discourse of marriage is central to the constitution of children's gendered and sexual subjectivities. Despite the broadening of marriage to include same-sex partnerships in many Western countries, the dominant and normative discourse is still marriage between a man and woman. This is reflected in children's mock wedding play scenarios, which generally continue to be strictly regulated heteronormative activities, replicating gendered power relations.

Children are not passive subjects in this process but are active agents constructing meanings around marriage and how it fits into their rights of passage (Robinson & Davies, 2015). Robinson and Davies (2015) point out that young children, despite their own family experiences, generally engage in a seemingly linear heteronormative narrative of life centrally featuring marriage: establishing relationships as boyfriend and girlfriends; dating; the man proposes; a wedding is planned; they go on a honeymoon, come back and live together; have a baby; and live together as a family 'forever'. The discourse of marriage, powerfully intersecting with the discourse of romantic love, for many children, legitimates love and intimate relationships (Robinson & Davies, 2015). The power of these discourses is that they permeate all aspects of children's conscious and unconscious lives (Foucault, 1974) – 'like osmosis' as one mother in Davies and Robinson's (2010) research stated. Butler's (1994) concept of performativity is core to understanding this process of how marriage, within a heteronormative framework, is central to the process of children's subjectification as gendered and sexual beings. This narrative and the heteronormative discourses that operate within it are naturalized (and often rendered invisible), through the ways it is repeatedly enacted by children in their everyday play interactions and dress-ups and through powerful adult and institutional reinforcements, children's literature, media and so on. The power of the discourse of marriage is intensified through the relationship between discourse and materiality. That is, the embodiment of the wedding experience: the desire, wearing the wedding attire, anticipating and feeling 'the kiss', the cutting of the cake, the dancing with your partner, the partying with friends and family – some of which children experience in their pretend play and at 'real' weddings.

Dress as a technology of power

As we have been arguing, dress is inextricable and critical to young children's construction of self as gendered (and sexual) subjects. Within a Foucaultian framework, we can see how clothing operates as a technology of power, organizing gendered bodies and regulating normative male–female binary gender. The following two excerpts from research with children demonstrate how bodies are controlled through gendered dress. In the first instance, a four-year-old girl Megan (from Jen's research), who is sitting happily eating a biscuit on the floor with her legs stretched out, suddenly notices that her dress has crept up her body showing her underwear. Jen recounts:

> Looking around her with a shade of embarrassment, she awkwardly pushes it down between her legs and tries to keep eating, but the skirt is so short that she can't hide her knickers, though she repeatedly tries. Eventually she curls her legs demurely underneath her to remedy the problem.

An eleven-year-old transgender girl, from research conducted by Robinson, Davies, Skinner, Ussher and Telfer (unpublished data), highlights how critical clothing is to her representation of gender expression. Clothing is core to being read as an intelligible gendered subject. In this case, the school uniform was being used by school authorities as a means through which to reinscribe and regulate gender intelligibility – a stable sex through a stable gender, as articulated by Butler's heterosexual matrix. Choosing what they wanted to wear was literally a matter of life and death for this young person:

> I love wearing the skirt and top; it makes me feel less inhibited, it makes me feel like me. I remember wearing the uniform for the first time; it was so exciting. I hated being forced to wear the boys' uniform; I really, really hated it and refused to keep doing it … If they continued making me do it I was going to kill myself, I hated it so much.

In contrasting the two data extracts, the multiplicity and complexity of experiencing school skirts are plainly seen; what is inhibiting for Megan's body, the skirt combining with gendered discourses of girlish appropriateness producing unnaturally curled-up limbs, is liberating for another, where the disconnect between subjectivity, emotions and the discourses evoked by boy-uniforms is extremely traumatizing. Discourse is not monolithic; children negotiate, take up, resist, dispute and transform enculturating influences and normalizing discourses they encounter in diverse ways that multiply across individual circumstance and experience.

Queering dress-ups: Transgressing discursive boundaries through the material embodiment of dress

The 'dress-up corner' is also a space in which some children feel safe and comfortable enough to challenge the boundaries of gender. It is a space where children can be somebody different, someone they would like to be, or a space where they can just be themselves. The 'dress-up corner' or other spaces created by children where they secretly, or otherwise, challenge gender norms through dress or dress-up can be viewed as 'queer spaces'. Robinson and Davies (2007) refer to queer spaces as those in which some children subvert dominant discourses of gender (and also childhood), doing gender differently. They point out that 'queer space refers to the place-making practices in which queer identities engage, as well as new spaces constructed by queer counter-publics' (2007: 21). Counter-publics are 'parallel discursive arenas where members of subordinated social groups invent and circulate counter discourses to formulate oppositional interpretations of their identities, interests, and needs' (Fraser, 1992: 123). Some children engage in counter-narratives of gender, sometimes in public, but often in private spaces away from the regulating gazes of other children or adults (Robinson & Davies, 2008a).

Children who transgress gender norms through dress-up in public spaces can encounter varying degrees of resistance from other children and adults. But what does 'queer dressing up' mean to some children? What does children's queer dressing up or 'cross-dressing' mean to educators, parents or other adults? Is it different for boys and girls? Tomboyism as a discursive sociocultural manifestation of gender and sexuality highlights the different ways in which masculinity can be taken up by female identified bodies (Blaise, 2005a; Halberstam, 1998; Paechter & Clark, 2007; Reay, 2001; Renold, 2005, 2006). Tomboys are usually understood as girls who take up traditionally masculine behaviours and interests that may be reflected through their more androgynous choice of clothing, for example

(Paechter & Clark, 2007). Girls have more freedom to experiment with gender fluidity and the taking up of masculinity, as pointed out previously by the cool-girls in Blaise's research, than boys' engagement with femininity. In the process of girls' performances of masculinity, they take up _some_ of the power associated with hegemonic masculinity – similar to women's 'power dressing', represented through wearing a suit. However, when girls' dressing up in androgynous or more masculine clothing persists into adolescence or adulthood, it raises concerns for some and presents questions about their sexuality (Paechter & Clark, 2007). Boys' transgressions of gender norms elicit more concern from other children and adults. This concern, particularly from other boys and boys' fathers, stems from the fear that this practice will lead to being gay in later life (Robinson & Davies, 2007).

Gender diverse and transgender children experience trauma from 'being dressed up' by parents/carers in clothing that is not representative of their preferred gender. They start experimenting with 'dressing up' in clothes representative of their preferred gender at early ages, often in private, when time and space provide opportunities to do so. Often acutely aware of the risks associated with transgressing gender norms through dress, beyond what is deemed socially acceptable for children in terms of gendered play, gender diverse and transgender children can find themselves in deep conflict with families and other adults or being taunted and ostracized by peers. This practice shifts beyond 'dressing up' experimentation to one of 'dressing' for survival – denying the agency of embodying their preferred gender, dress being the critical marker of this, can lead to serious depression and suicide ideation for these children and young people. Gender diverse and transgender children (youths and adults) highlight the critical importance of the embodiment of one's preferred gender expression; the discourse they often articulate is being 'born in the wrong body'.

Jack Halberstam's work on female masculinity and queer time and space has been significant to queer theorizing of the fluidity of gender, gender as performance, and in understanding childhood as a queer time and space (1998, 2005). Halberstam critiques the perpetuation of the binary gender system, man/woman, pointing out that it fails to address the multiple performances of male and female that exist across bodies. The female born person who is consistently read as not female demonstrates the inadequacy and instability of the category woman. Within this binary gender system, masculinity is rigidly associated with the male body, not a performance of gender that is also produced and sustained across female bodies. As pointed out by Cristyn Davies (2008), Halberstam is concerned with revealing as fictional the _essential_ relation between male bodies and masculinity. Halberstam's aim is to denaturalize the discourse of masculinity, demonstrating its performative dimension, and to create a discursive space in which masculinity can be read in relation to the female body (Davies, 2008). Halberstam argues that masculinity is not the sole domain of men, proposing an alternative to compulsory binary gender, suggesting a system of 'gender preference', which allows for gender neutrality until children and young adults 'announce his or her or its gender' (1998: 27). Halberstam suggests that one could 'come out' as a gender in a similar fashion to coming out in sexuality. However, as it stands, those who do not fit into the compulsory gender binary are often pathologized and highlighted through medical discourses that have labelled some children as having gender identity disorder of childhood (Butler, 2004a; Sedgwick, 1990). Bronwyn Davies (1989: 235) points out that children's agency in challenging rigid gender binaries and taking up non-normative performances of gender 'involves grappling with both subjective constraints and the constraints of accepted discursive practices'. Cheryl Kilodavis (2009), a mother of a four-year-old boy, who loved dressing up in a princess outfit, authored the children's book, '*My Princess Boy: A mom's story about a young boy who loved to dress up*'. 'As a community', Kilodavis comments, 'we can accept and support our children for whomever they are and however they wish to look' (npn). The following is a short excerpt from Kilodavis's book:

> I love my Princess Boy. When we go shopping he is happiest when looking at girls clothes. But when he says he wants to buy a pink bag or sparkly dress, people stare at him. And when he buys girl things, they laugh at him, and then they laugh at me. It hurts us both.

In concluding this section of the chapter, we are mindful that the shift to post-humanism poses some important questions, in particular, in terms of its relationship with FPS, queer theory, the queering of gender binaries and the 'plasticity' of gendered and sexed bodies. What new insights are to be gained by shifting the focus onto (human and non-human) bodies themselves? As queerness is powerfully embodied, post-humanism may be able to provide a lens through which to capture the affective implications of queer bodies more effectively.

Feminist post-structuralism and feminist post-humanism: Radical departures or beneficial alliances?

Despite the prominence of feminist theorists in the collective development of post-humanism, such as Haraway, Braidotti, and Barad, the uptake of this group of theories within the feminist academy has been met with a substantial amount of resistance based on its potential conflict with preceding and alternative feminist approaches. A portion of this resistance appears, through personal encounters, to be based on a common misapprehension regarding post-humanism and its relationship to post-structuralism: that it purports to *replace* a focus on discourse and power with one of bodies and fluidity. This error is exacerbated by the disconcerting challenge to neo-liberal humanism it presents, which dislodges the subject (including, commonly, the reader/researcher themselves) from their own rationalized, culturally and historically informed narrative and perceived experience as a separate individual moving in a linear fashion through space and time. A sense of affront is understandable when one's own lived experience is reframed in such a radical manner, and indeed the very name of 'post-humanism' is itself inherently provocative to humans engaging with it. This evokes the spectre of opposition that emerged over post-structuralism, the terming of which implied to many to form a complete revocation of structuralism where, in fact, the exact nature of their differences and similarities continues to be debated productively by feminist theorists (Davies, 1997; Jones, 1993). The provocation and overt radicalism of post-humanist frameworks can obscure the *inclusion* of discourse, power, ethics of response/ability (as Barad terms it) and the humanized experience of being a boundaried subject within a range of loosely collected frameworks that expand the range of possible relations available to beings and bodies, rather than limiting them. Davies (2016) provides a clear and useful discussion of the distinctions between post-structuralism and post-humanism, and the only clear breaks she identifies between the two paradigms are post-humanism's withdrawal from representationalism and the disavowal of the separate, knowing, analytical researcher, standing apart from the phenomenon they are seeking to understand. Here, Davies identifies those aspects of post-humanism troubling to those feminist researchers who have engaged deeply with post-humanism and find serious concerns as a result of that considered interrogation.

The gains made within a representational feminist framework regarding the study of marginalization and oppression have been significant; however, Barad offers a reworking of the subjectivity concept that underpins it. The core difference here stems from Barad's alteration of agency as 'an enactment and not something someone has' (2007: 214), with cause and effect emerging from dynamic material-discursive configurations, rather than being a matter of social power distribution and exertion. In these terms alone, her proposal seems troubling in that it appears to remove accountability for inequalities and oppression by locating them 'beyond the human'. If agency is not possessed and exerted by the human subject, how then can we promote the agency of the marginalized, let alone critique the actions of dominant social groups or individuals? There is, however, adequate scope within agential-realism for accountability and human responsibility, but Barad urges us to contextualize these features within broader contexts than a single individual or sociocultural group.

In Barad's proposal, humans do not have different forms of agency in their possession but are agentially constituted as subjects and objects through the material-discursive 'apparatus' with which they are entangled. This apparatus, in terms of social inequalities, includes historical, cultural, geographical, economic and spatial conditions among others too numerous to name. The exact temporal nature of this material-discursive apparatus (of which, crucially, the human is a part) in any given context enacts an 'agential cut' between entities that delineates their subject and object, as well as their 'cause' and 'effect' status. What we then perceive as localized (human) agency, she locates as produced meanings regarding relations (including human inequalities) that are based on a particular arrangement or configuring of the material-discursive world, including humanity who are 'responsible for the world of which we are a part, not because it is an arbitrary construction of our choosing but because reality is sedimented out of particular practices that we have a role in shaping and through which we are shaped' (2007: 390). These practices can be located in our 'knowings' of the world – the meanings we produce that in themselves are material engagements, creating 'differences that matter' (2007: 381) that shape us and that we are shaped by. Importantly, (re)configurings of the world are iterative: 'phenomena are forever being re-enfolded and reformed' (2007: 177). In this way, longitudinal phenomena of inequality, such as sexism or racism, can achieve an exponential velocity *even as the possibility for disruption or change is always present*. Therefore, not only is human accountability and responsibility for inequalities present in agential-realism, albeit only with reference to other entangled material-discursive bodies, but also present are radical possibilities for reconfiguration to produce alternative phenomena, which could change inequalities. The primary issue that obfuscates the implications of this argument for accountability and responsibility is perhaps Barad's unwieldy contextualization within real-world contexts within her core text. Choosing to explore these implications largely through obscure techno-scientific phenomena that few readers will have previously encountered, it is often challenging to relate her arguments to the social issues that concern representationalist feminist politics; her discussion of 'fetal agency' is arguably the most relatable illustration of her themes (2007: 215–220).

Some further prominent critique regarding the construction of post-humanism centres around an argued *misapprehension of post-structuralism* as somehow 'anti-matter' and over-focused on language. Ahmed critiques the immanent radicalism in Barad's striking 2003 manifesto for a 'posthumanist performativity' (now swept into a strand of thought known as 'new materialism' and referenced as such in Ahmed's piece):

> This caricature of poststructuralism as matter-phobic involves a rather mournful lament: a call for a return to the facts of the matter ... By turning matter into an object or theoretical category, in this way, the new materialism reintroduces the binarism between materiality and culture that much work in science studies has helped to challenge. Matter becomes a fetish object: as if it can be an 'it' that we can be for or against. (Ahmed, 2008: 34–35)

Despite her robust concerns, Ahmed ultimately reaches the same conclusion regarding feminist post-humanism/new materialism that Davies comes to eight years later – that regardless of the excitement and invigoration that a potential paradigm shift evokes, we should be deeply suspicious of making claims of departure and 'newness' about an approach that implicitly and overtly stands on the shoulders of the 'prior'. The acknowledgement of this debt is echoed in Barad's own later writings: 'The past was never simply there to begin with and the future is not simply what will unfold; the "past" and the "future" are iteratively reworked and enfolded' (Barad, 2010: 260–261). With these arguments in mind, it may be more logical to consider these feminist approaches and others neither as separate entities with their own characteristics nor as even consecutive chapters in some boundless narrative of feminist academia, but rather as inscribed sheets of acetate, which, while apparently able to be read alone, only in layering can fully illuminate the dis/continuous reworking and enfolding nature of feminist approaches to bodies, time, space, matter and – indeed – discourse.

If this layering approach is adopted as a feminist post-humanism that incorporates and builds on, rather than replaces, post-structuralism, what then can it add to the above 'pure' post-structuralist interpretation of children's dress/dressing-up encounters with clothing? What more can we understand about the layering of clothing through the acetate layering of feminist theory and research practices, and do our interpretations recast the very experience of 'dressing-up' as one of a distinct, boundaried gendered-child-subject as we undercut the notion of the boundaried, singular feminist-researcher-subject?

Putting post-humanism to work on dress/dressing-up data

If we explore dress and dressing-up data with feminist post-humanism, rather than post-structuralism, we ask different questions of the data to produce meaning, primarily focusing on bodies and materiality, with discourse as a background presence. In the above analysis that applies Foucault and what can be adequately – if reductively – described as the 'post-structural Butler', the focus of analysis is on the implications of children's agency and their drive to experiment and queer dress to explore their subjectivities. Here, our analytic terminology is drawn from Barad's framework and terminology, though the core concepts of decentralizing the humanist subject and dislocating possessive agency can be similarly exerted through the work of other post-humanist theorists. This configures our discussion to centre around the entangled relations between children and clothing within the material-discursive conditions of the world that relate to gender, sexuality, clothing and childhood. We focus on material effects in the (re)configuring of the world, rather than discursive lineage, and on consequences rather than causes, while also exploring the shape of the world in which these intra-actions occur and child-gendering 'becomings' emerge. We ask not 'why' but 'how' gender happens and consider not what was intended (a working of possessive agency) but on what was experienced, as agency flows through bodies. The excitement of the post-humanist approach is a further disruption to stability and permanence, as it centralizes the fragility and instability of identity and, by locating it as performative, carries an inherent possibility for reshaping rigid, binary gender as a phenomenon and as a knowledge.

We can see this analytic approach demonstrated by Mazzei (2013) with regard to adult experiences of dress and dressing up, and her discussion is useful to evoke here. Mazzei draws on the notion of 'viscous porosity' introduced by Tuana (2008) in order to conceptualize the relationship between human bodies and transformative clothing, in that instance, a student (named 'Sera') and a suit. She gains insight from Tuana's suggestion that all boundaries between objects, bodies, discourses and concepts are permeable, separated by membranes rather than solid lines, and that 'once the molecular interaction occurs, there is no divide between nature/culture, natural/artificial ... there are important migrations between and across these divides that can be occluded by efforts to posit a dualism' (2008: 202). In the case of Sera and the suit, their 'wearing entanglement' melded the human and non-human in the co-production of professionalism and confidence. Mazzei observes that this blurring of separable beings demonstrates the usefulness of 'thinking diffractively' with Barad: seeing the entanglement of human bodies and clothing in productive intra-activity thwarts the limitations of thinking of human bodies as bounded by skin and prompts us to consider how we become subject in- and outside the material body. Developing this analytic theme, Taylor observes that 'clothes as materialities *become* with us as we *become* with them in an open, contingent unfolding of mattering' (2013: 699, italics ours), and this concept of 'becoming' within intra-action can act as an anchor for considering lived experiences of gender through clothing. It is not simply that clothing makes us something else but that our entanglement with clothing opens up possibilities to produce meaning and experiences for both ourselves and that clothing in a reconfiguring of our material-discursive world. Clothing is not simply transformative of the body itself but of the world-in-becoming around that body, into its pasts and into its futures. While outfits are frequently changed, their transformative effects on the gendering of the world cannot be effectively boundaried by that term 'dressing-up', which evokes a fleeting occasion to be experienced and then abandoned. There can be no forgetting in the dis/continuity of feminist post-humanism, where momentary experiences become a constellation of sharpened experiential points that come to define interpretation of a life in more acetate layers of subjectivity.

Juelskjaer (2013) terms these epitomical points of knowledge and experience 'subjectivations', a term with roots in Barad's agential cutting 'together-apart' of subject and object in a manifestation of material-discursive conditions. Here, meaning is produced through (re)determining the permeable boundary of the body and the other bodies with which it is entangled: the material of clothes unworn and worn, the congealed-yet-still-dynamic heteronormative discourses of appearance, the private or the public space, the historical moment where 'queer' and 'gay' reference more than oddness and joy. Locating the becoming of the human subject within this apparatus, its subjectivation, is an effective way of discussing how lived human experience and knowledge are produced within the complex web of materiality and discourse, time and space. When bodies and clothes become entangled in gender production, the subjectivations they produce can only be articulated or understood in relation to all other material and discursive entanglements in which they are simultaneously, previously or potentially involved. To break this down even further, the experiences, body and character of each person, and of each outfit, and of each space and time in which outfits are worn matter for the particular gender articulation produced in each intra-action. When Mazzei thinks through the intra-action of Sera and the suit and what it produces, she meticulously rakes through not only her and Sera's experiences of professionalism, confidence and clothing, but also the recent history of suits and female bodies – thinking about the Thatcherite 'power dressing' of the 1980s – in order to locate Sera's specific subjectivation when interpellated by the suit. Such analysis of connection and multiplicity enables a cartographic understanding of subjective enactments that, while intensely complex in its relationality, offers a realistic chance of comprehending the conditions of producing gender as experienced by material-discursive subjects.

As with adult clothing, child/clothing entanglements always draw from a citational chain that is deeply, inextricably interlinked with gender and sexuality – there can be no material meeting of child and clothing without the concept of gender and, therefore, sexuality demanding attention. As we saw in the above extract featuring Megan and her too-short skirt, even very young children are able and willing to alter their bodies to suit the demands of heteronormative gender. In that 'everyday clothing' example, Megan's predicament articulates the double-bind at the very heart of gender-based inequality: the shape of the skirt when combined with the discursive knowledge of hetero-femininity demands that her clothing simultaneously reveals and conceals her body in order for it to be socially acceptable. While a feminist post-structuralist lens prompts us to consider the discourses of femininity and childhood that are at work shaping Megan's body and her clothing, feminist post-humanism asks us *also* to carefully attend to the specific apparatus of production and the material features of Megan's body and the skirt, as well as the playground, the preschool and even the biscuit that she holds in her hand. In this framing, we can not only see *why* Megan curls up her legs to hide her knickers but also track the specific intra-actions that are cut to produce a knowing of carelessness, of femininity, and ultimately, of shame and necessity for physical self-correction. This perspective exposes additional opportunities for intervention and change to be sought beyond the discursive that may otherwise be missed or obscured (Lyttleton-Smith, 2017).

To explore this in a different example, here we turn to a scenario not of everyday dress but of 'dressing-up' in the early years setting – a moment where normative expectations are overtly set aside yet still have a vital role to play in the human experience of wearing 'other' clothes.

> From the moment Christopher slips into his outfit, he is calmer, more relaxed, the feather-boa tickling his neck, while his hands move slowly back and forth over the soft silky dark blue fabric. He doesn't notice the other children grabbing at their costumes or scavenging for gems through the leftover discarded clothes in the big red dress-up box. (Robinson's data)

This extract captures a delicate intra-action between fabric material and human skin where the sensuality of sensitive touch is linked directly with emotions of tranquillity and an almost meditative sense of peace. The central bodies within this entanglement merge together easily and willingly; they *slip* and *tickle* pleasantly, and hands massage the inviting fabric, pressing it closer to skin than mere wearing achieves. This language, both in extract and analysis, clearly evokes sexuality, and this is not accidental: two bodies – clothing and Christopher – have come together in a way that is both pleasurable and private, as the peripheral apparatus of other children and other clothes are contrasted in their aggressive *grabbing* and *scavenging*. The impression of an ethereal, deeply personal experience is created in its distinction from the animalistic chaos implied around Christopher's contentedly swathed body. Thinking here with Tuana's 'viscous porosity', Christopher's skin is so tangibly permeable that the intra-activity becomes less of a *wearing* and more of a *melding* as each body becomes-together, the feathers and silkiness liberated from the brash, messy jumble of the dressing-up box, and the human body and emotion freed from the movement and commotion that surrounds it. As with Sera and her suit, a meaning emerges quite clearly from this extract that is couched in the material-discursive apparatus that produces it: we know that little boys are not supposed to appreciate sensuality and stillness; however, we do not *only* know this from discourse but also from the contrast between the melded clothing-Christopher body and the multiple other outfit-child bodies that orbit it. The meaning, then, that becomes apparent to a reader interested in gender and childhood is one of *queerness*, as normative childhood gender is deviated, and yet *naturalness*, as the comfort and peace of the clothing-Christopher body pose its direct challenge to this normativity in such a way that the cheating-away from boys of subtle bodily enjoyment untarnished by notions of 'correct' gender/sexuality is exposed, its artifice and deceit apparent.

For adherence to agential-realism, it is important here to refrain from casting this incident as some kind of 'turning point' or permanent transformation for Christopher, as this implies a linear, progressive notion of time and personhood that is not accommodated within a Baradian or broader post-humanist framework. Instead we might consider the features of the subjectivation that emerges here and its difference to the other potential subjectivations that are seemingly being experienced by other children around Christopher. This understanding is of neither a singular or completely transformative shift that instigates a new identity nor an entirely temporal, fleeting occurrence that passes on the separation of the human and non-human bodies that are entangled. Rather, it forms one articulation of a subject of 'multiple belongings, as a relational subject constituted in and by multiplicity ... a subject that works across differences and is also internally differentiated' (Braidotti, 2013: 49). Here, the clothing-Christopher body is both coherent and dissonant with its current entanglement: coherent, for here is a boy playing with clothing within a presented dressing-up context just as the other children are, and yet dissonant, as the difference of his experience compared to the other children is clear. From this apparent contradiction, a new material-discursive possibility emerges for both Christopher *and* the other children: another way for a body to be 'dressed' and another way for a body to be gendered.

The frisson of dissonance: Dress-up, emotion and becoming

In this section, we explore the simultaneous multiple-belongings of dressing-up experiences and how they produce contradictions internally and externally to the human bodies featured in our data. We begin here with an outfit of everyday dress for one body, which becomes a costume when melded with another.

> [Girl's jeans] weren't cool like her brother's jeans. Alex loved to pull the thick blue denim jeans up over her hips, which quickly disappeared in the bagginess of the pants. The red flannelette shirt matched the jeans perfectly, she thought. She slipped her hands into the front pockets, turning from side to side to see her image. Alex liked what it looked like. She looked different, felt different, stronger, taller and more confident. Grabbing her brother's boots from his room, she slipped them on. They almost fitted; they were only a couple of sizes too big. The outfit was finished now. (Robinson's data)

In this extract, distinct and explicitly 'different' emotions emerge from the meeting of materially masculine clothes and Alex's young female body. A frisson of dissonance permeates the entanglement that does not just 'appear to others' but appears to something deep inside the self. As with Christopher's dressing up, the melding feels 'right' in its contradiction of Alex's disappearing hips and too-small feet. In post-structuralism, this could be analysed as a 'power grab', where young femininity reappropriates masculine discourses of strength and confidence, but post-humanism prompts us to focus on the materiality of the entanglement. Alex's thoughts quite clearly demonstrate a viscous porosity as these senses appear to seep from the fabric through her skin to emerge in her emotions. For Alex, the bagginess, the thickness, the large size and heaviness of boots – these are not simply 'markers' of masculinity; they have a physical impact that interacts with skin and muscle, loosening the constraints that tight feminine jeans and shoes impose on bodies. The clothes themselves undertake their own transformation beyond Alex's emotions: they do not simply become 'girls clothes' but achieve presence in an intermediate queer place which dislocates them from the discourses that informed their initial cutting and stitching. Meanwhile, Alex's 'old' body, before her brother's clothes merged with it, has quite literally disappeared and the new clothing-Alex body becomes together as physically more free and more powerful, her limbs embracing enhanced movement and the thick fabric shielding them from cold and touch.

There is a touch of the superhero identity-switch here – of Clark Kent/ Superman emerging from a phone booth, becoming more powerful than moments before and raising the question of 'true identity'; is it the suit he wears more frequently or the Lycra he wears more freely? For the clothing-Alex body, it is the irresolution of this query where the significance of this dress-up emerges. If Alex's body were not marked as 'female' and the clothing body not marked as 'male', the moment of dress would be unremarkable, and the feelings of strength and confidence either would not emerge or would appear quite differently than they do here. The realized potential for clothing-Alex to be both dressed and 'dressed-up', masculine and female, is what imbues the intra-action with such excitement and pleasure.

Thus far, we have explored private moments of dress, where the implied or actual presence of others (the unwritten group of children around Megan, the visible children around Christopher, the comparative image of Alex's brother she evokes) has not yet intruded on the melding of single human bodies with outfits. The becomings emerge from two material bodies together-alone, and the knowledges of others only indirectly intervene within these extracts. In the next extract, we follow what happens in a preschool classroom when a private moment of dressing up becomes public through direct encounters with other bodies.

> The children experiment with encountering fearful situations through the monster and wild animal games. The exertions of power that the instigating child experiences are usually satisfyingly successful for them, as a monster game very rarely falls flat. This afternoon, Ethan has put on the wolf costume and engaged an unusually large number of children in the game. About six children … come running into the home corner and hide behind the kitchen units, squealing. But Ethan is not a very scary wolf and apart from a rather quiet growl and his

This book marks a new departure in academic scholarship. It considers the ways in which feminist poststructuralist scholars have made vital contributions to shifting understandings of children, childhood, gender and sexualities and explores continuities and discontinuities with new materialist and posthumanist approaches. It is meticulous in explaining earlier work, bringing rare lucidity and analytic clarity to the task. This, in itself, would make it an invaluable reference for academics and students. *Feminists Researching Gendered Childhoods: Generative Entanglements* does much more than this, however. It traces lines through feminist research, examining how feminist researchers have employed poststructuralist, new materialist and posthumanist theories in generative ways to illuminate children's intersectional engagement with gender and sexuality. In the best feminist traditions, it draws on collaboration and discussion as methods of engaging with novelty and crafting the new from deep, respectful understandings of previous thinking. The result is a text that will shift readers' theoretical and practical understanding of everyday social inequities and power relations in childhood in the service of promoting social justice. It breathes new life into the notion of 'situated knowledge'.

Ann Phoenix, Professor of Psychosocial Studies, Thomas Coram Research Unit, UCL Institute of Education, University College London, UK

How gender matters in the field of early childhood is in need of some response-able, radical re-assembling as gender as concept and event is becoming increasingly undone and troubling. Staying with the trouble, this curious collection of chapters from established and emergent queer and feminist educational scholars does just that. Every page offers up a range of speculative entanglements to get stuck into/with, re-mattering how knowledge about gender in early childhood is fielded and produced through some familiar and unfamiliar post-structuralist, new materialist and posthuman frames. Dive in, and intra-act with some extra-ordinary and lively encounters that will keep the field and what we 'do' with our 'doings', lively, mattering and ethical.

Emma Renold, Professor of Childhood Studies, School of Social Sciences, Cardiff University, UK

What is particularly interesting about this book is how it re-turns to and foregrounds the complexity of how gender is produced in early childhood – and not just by humans, but through what Jane Bennett calls "vibrant matter" (e.g., Lego blocks, moving bodies, dressing up clothes). When reading the chapters diffractively through one another gendered binaries are queered – offering an imaginary of post-developmental research practices that move beyond words through the corporeal sensing of material-discursive entanglements. The authors' message is clear throughout: decentering the human in new materialism does not mean a break with poststructuralism or an erasure of gender. On the contrary, fresh connections are made and the new ideas work generatively to produce equitable and transformative pedagogies – always with an eye on honouring past feminist poststructuralist research. With a clear commitment to doing justice to the 'inbetween' of human and more-than-human in early childhood gender studies, this book is a timely response to critics who argue that posthumanists try to erase humanist concerns, such as race, gender, class and ability. What the book argues for is that new materialism is not 'new', but always already entangled with 'the' past and a useful section traces some of these entanglements.

Karin Murris, Professor, University of Cape Town, South Africa

This stunning landmark of collaborative feminist writing embodies generative feminisms in both content and design. *Feminists Researching Gendered Childhoods*, creatively led and innovatively co-edited by Jayne Osgood and Kerry Robinson, pushes against traditional practices of assembling edited volumes. Thinking with, and building on, the new materialist/affective turn in feminist scholarship on gender and sexualities in childhood, this groundbreaking book brings together a new generation of prominent feminist scholars whose 'generative entanglements' recognize the shifting and (extra)ordinarily specific contexts in which everyday events in early childhood play out. It is not simply in the stunning writing that a proactive new ethic, from which to generate a multi-layered means towards rethinking gender and childhood, is put to work: it is also in their illuminating performance of collaboration in writing that the contributing authors uniquely position themselves, applying various theorists – including Sara Ahmed, Karen Barad, Rosi Braidotti, Judith Butler and Donna Haraway, amongst others – and their concepts to provoke and inspire new research in the field of gender and early childhood. This is more than a germinal text for childhood research: it offers us a way of changing how we see childhood; of changing how we address each other's writing; of changing how we understand and engage with feminist new materialist modes of enquiry; and of changing ourselves, to take courage, challenge and keep questioning and unsettling the assumptions we hold about gender and childhood.

Pamela Burnard, Professor of Arts, Creativities and Education,
University of Cambridge, UK

This book offers a strong and timely collection of writings that invites readers to renew attention to how matter comes to matter in the production of gender in early childhood spaces. As a new comer to new materialisms this book offers a challenge to stay with and wrestle with the complexities and dis-continuities in how childhood has been theorised and researched. This book is a must-read for anyone navigating a way into the new materiailsms and working out how to put it into practice.

Sid Mohandas, Early Childhood Teacher, PhD Student,
Founder of *The Male Montessorian,* UK

clawing fingers held by his face he seems unsure of how to develop his persona. He stands a metre or so away from the children on the other side of the units, and when children run past him – either to join in or escape – he lets them pass without challenge. (Jen's data)

Under normal circumstances, quiet and reclusive four-year-old Ethan exerts no dominance or aggression in the classroom, often fading into the background or hiding away in quiet corners to relax by himself. He talks very little, and when he does, it is almost a whisper, the effort of it seeming to drain him emotionally. Though he is tall, he is slender and moves with gentleness and delicacy, and the games he prefers are caring or family role play scenarios, often with girls rather than boys. The dissonance of the felted wolf costume with Ethan's everyday character is striking. Yet, somehow, merged with the costume, Ethan becomes a figure of power, single-handedly instigating a widespread monster game through almost no further action beyond his distinctly unferocious growl and stiff, curled fingers. What is remarkable here is how this agential power operating through the wolf costume sidelines any historical context that the other children might associate with Ethan. Even he does not seem to understand it, reacting with uncertainty to the other children's delighted enactments of terror. All the active work to produce fear and excitement in the game is now being performed by other children. Ethan's human body with its quietness and timidity seems to be absent here, and in its place only wolf-Ethan remains.

If we think with post-structuralism here, something seems a little awry; is Ethan agentially drawing from and renegotiating discourses of gender to gain social power that he otherwise could not grasp? If so, he seems unaware of this power being in his possession, apparently surprised by the force with which his activity impacts the social group. Perhaps we can return usefully to Barad whose formulation of agency may better capture the power dynamics at play in this specific extract than a Foucaultian reading can. Above, we referenced Barad's conception of agency as 'an enactment and not something someone has' (2007: 214), dislodging power from individual human intent and locating it as working through a dynamic material-discursive apparatus; cutting subjects and objects as it flows; and channelling that power through bodies, both human and non-human, to produce what we can observe, in this instance, as play-aggression and, subsequently, mock-terror. The knowing 'subject' in this data is not the wolf-Ethan body (though it may become so in the next instance or even in an alternative reading of the same instance) but the other children who read it, producing meaning, and react to their knowledge, producing it as fearful even as it flounders in its own effects. The agency belongs to the monster game – its history, joy, infectiousness and boisterousness – and seems to jump off wolf-Ethan almost immediately to transfer to the other human bodies surrounding it, creating sparks of movement and sound as it passes through. We can certainly return to post-structuralism to explore what is happening discursively here, again centralizing Ethan-as-subject and considering the implications of gender and early childhood discourse criss-crossing this subjectivity, but applying the post-humanist perspective here has illuminated something new and vital about how a costume becomes visible to others and produces social effects (or becomings) beyond the individual body.

A feminist in post-humanist clothing? Multilayering feminist theory as childhood researchers

Feminist post-structuralism offers understandings of what discursive 'rules' are adhered to and broken, while post-humanism enables a perspective on exactly how and why this is the case in a given scenario/phenomenon. We have found post-humanism to be most effectively used not as a replacement for analyses of power and discourse but as an additional layer of analysis that enhances the post-structural/post-humanist. We argue that there is no need or benefit to adopting wholesale paradigm change and far more to be gained by applying concepts from each paradigm to critique and illuminate each other. Furthermore, the current internal and public discomforts engaged in by some feminist sociologists of gender, including ourselves, regarding who we 'really' are as researchers as we meld with and break from theoretical costumes, can obscure our capacity to experience Braidotti's 'multiple belongings' in our analytic work and our research identities.

Our feminist post-humanist analysis of childhood clothing encounters prompts a distinctive perspective on the data that clearly builds on the initial feminist post-structuralist analysis that we presented. Where the Foucaultian analysis took us on an analytic journey through discourses of power and heteronormativity and through the social institution of marriage and its discursive performativity, we now also have an eye trained on the emotions and sensations that occur when these discourses emerge within material, lived experience. Some may argue that the interpretations in this analysis would be achievable through post-structuralist frameworks, and perhaps they are right. Indeed, this could be true of any theoretical framework; if we just thought long enough and wrote hard enough, we could draw from data, any data, the interpretations we do without reference to any theorist or their abstract, adaptive lexicon. What is useful about theory is it provides questions to ask of data that we may not otherwise consider, and through the sedimented expertise and refinement of repeated application by disparate colleagues of varied interest, space and time, it encourages us down pathways of thought that we may not otherwise have noticed, let alone explored. The grand boulevard of feminist post-structuralism can still stand strong, as academically and politically vital as the past thirty years of feminist researchers have found it to be, as we continue to explore this newer, winding, branching path of feminist post-humanism that weaves around and through it.

5

Materialized Reconfigurations of Gender in Early Childhood: Playing Seriously with Lego

Jayne Osgood

I return, again I reach up, take down a book from my son's shelf, on the way, there or back – I am not sure which, I wince a familiar wince as I prise a 2x2 Lego brick from the arch of my foot, I go to my study I ponder, I remember, I wonder, I write ….

Following on from the previous, this chapter takes a material object that is routinely and habitually found in childhood contexts, across the globe, to reconfigure ideas about gender. The chapter insists that taking matter seriously, in this case the humble Lego brick, can produce both recognizable accounts about gender and also hold the potential to open up ideas and take investigations in unanticipated directions. This chapter works with Haraway's (2016) SF philosophy, notably her method of string figuring, and her concern to tell stories via methods of speculative fabulation. By endeavouring to tell different and multiple stories about Lego, this chapter re-turns to a range of disciplinary fields and theoretical orientations, including feminist post-structuralism, to consider how gender is understood, assessed and produced in early childhood contexts through Lego. This chapter seeks to address a number of guiding questions, namely how have childhood materials been theorized over time, through different feminist theoretical lenses? And therefore, what claims have been made? What policy, curricular, pedagogical advances, regressions and stagnations have occurred? What do new materialist feminist approaches to the study of gender in childhood, which take matter as a starting point, offer to existing debates?

Block play

> I'm pretty sure I always had LEGO bricks to play with. I think they must have
> belonged to my older sisters and brothers. We kept them in an old baby bath,
> and I remember always rummaging around in it looking for the parts I needed
> to build. However, when I was 13 my brother sold all the family LEGO pieces so
> I was without it for many years. I have only started building again in the last five
> years. (Andrew Walker, 45, UK in Lipkowitz, 2011)

Materiality, how matter comes to matter and the mattering of matter, is a
matter of concern to new materialist feminists researching early childhood.
As outlined in the opening chapters to this book, there has been a shift in
emphasis from the primacy of the human subject in childhood research,
a shift that demands research methodologies are reconfigured so that the
relationship between theory and practice might be rethought (Holmes et al.,
2018; Lenz-Taguchi, 2010). It demands that we grapple with the inseparability
of thinkingfeelingdoing to move beyond representationalism, that is, capturing
what is reflected back to us and then reporting on it; instead we can consider
the generative possibilities presented within research investigations to produce
new knowledges and ways of being in the world. Feminist new materialists
argue that research holds the potential to be more productive than is often the
case; by recognizing ourselves as entangled within research practices demands
that we cultivate a heightened sense of response-ability (Barad, 2007; Haraway,
2008). Working with a concern to engage with how knowledge is materially-
discursively produced and by resisting the urge to distinguish between past and
present, nature and culture, feminist researchers are offered a mode of enquiry
that is productive and therefore that might set us free from getting stuck in
familiar ways of thinking and ways of doing research. Approaching the study of
gender in early childhood from this position reshapes understandings of what
data might be (Lather & St Pierre, 2013; MacLure, 2013), what research becomes
and the importance of embracing the never-endingness of a 'radical curiosity'
(Haraway, 2016: 37); it demands a need for constant thoughtfulness about our
decentred place in the world.

> My finished models rarely look anything like my initial idea – I just go with the
> flow, really, and let the model itself dictate how it's going to look! (Barney Main,
> 18, UK in Lipkowitz, 2011: 36)

A new materialist researcher sensibility owes an enormous debt to feminist
research from the 1970s and 1980s that argued for reciprocity and the need

to write ourselves into the research situation. And yet further indebtedness to intersectional and post-structuralist approaches taken by feminist researchers in the 1980s and 1990s which insisted our situated place within research was significant, and a resource to enable us to critically and self-consciously engage with accounts gathered through research in subjective and deeply invested ways. However, the material and affective were regarded as secondary to the human subject in these investigations, and this is where the distinction lies. For feminist new materialists, the objective is to bring the human, non-human and more-than-human into investigations giving them equal weight but retaining a feminist conviction to the goals underpinning research. This willingness to work with flattened ontologies opens out what research looks like and what gets brought into the frame.

Haraway (2016) stresses that the greatest danger we face is thoughtlessness; working within new materialist feminist frameworks insists upon heightened thoughtfulness. Research invites us to become wayfarers and to recognize ourselves as intrinsically entangled in that which we are concerned to research. Through our research experiments and investigations, boundaries become more blurry (about what counts as 'data', the claims that can be made, the goal(s) of our investigations). Research becomes more like an adventure, starting in the middle

Image 5.1 What it is is beautiful. Source: https://www.themarysue.com/girl-in-old-lego-ad/

and being open to uncertainty and surprises. The goal becomes to track lines and all the while cultivate response-ability and recognize our place within the world, and to recognize the world-making possibilities that are present within each encounter. This mode of enquiry creates opportunities to reconfigure both practices and ideas; it is dynamic and creative, uncertain and surprising. It pushes us to think more expansively and to think the unthought. It offers possibilities to break free from sedimented ways of knowing and being and to imagine (and produce) other worlds. By working to reconfigure established ideas, structures, practices and policies in early childhood contexts that inform what we think we know about gender, the familiar becomes strange and so offers generative possibilities to think about issues such as gender in early childhood in other ways.

> Nothing is impossible with LEGO bricks! … If you can't figure it out, step back for a bit, do something else and go back later. (Duncan Titmarsh, 40, UK in Lipkowitz, 2011: 164)

With this in mind, this chapter takes an embodied and experimental approach towards thinkingfeelingdoing which recognizes the world as fluid, ongoing and excessive (Lorimer, 2005). New materialist frameworks offer a relational understanding of the world (people, nature, things, time and space) where non-human entities also have a capacity to affect and participate in sense-making. Pyyry (2016: 103) writes about enchantment, which she argues becomes possible when one engages with environments and encounters that open up questions about routine everyday practices, things and ways of being. Enchantment makes the familiar unfamiliar, or as Bennett (2001: 4) stresses: 'To be enchanted is to be struck and shaken by the extraordinary that lives amid the familiar and the everyday.' This chapter takes the Lego brick (something familiar, everyday, seemingly unremarkable and commonplace in many childhoods) as a source of enchantment and a means to reconfigure understandings about gender in early childhood:

> *The starting point of all LEGO models is the LEGO brick. The basic LEGO Brick has two simple components: studs on one side, tubes on the other. The studs of one brick lock into the tubes of another. The LEGO Group call this 'clutch power'! LEGO bricks come in many shapes and sizes but all bricks have the ability to connect to another.* (Lipkowitz, 2011: 4)

The plastic brick offers something to think with but more than that something to live with (Haraway, 2003). The affective forces of the Lego brick generate surprises and changes of direction in what we might thinkfeeldo about gender in early childhood.

String figuring लेगो לגו லெகோ لیگو樂高レゴ인사고 تركيب لگو
العاب лего乐高

Inspired by Haraway, this chapter attempts to weave a cat's cradle of different cultural representations of human relations with Lego from educational psychology, neo-liberal capitalism, scientific manufacturing and environmental activism to research experiments in order to acknowledge our response-ability to engage with ideas that gender is reconfigured through Lego and that ultimately gender in childhood is much more than only an human(ist) matter. Haraway (2008) offers a pragmatic, poetic and playfully serious guide to an ethics and politics committed to recognizing human relationality and entanglement. Working with Haraway's SF philosophy requires excavation, provocation and 'deep hanging out' (2016). This chapter works with archival and visual research methodologies so that the aesthetic aspects of naturecultures might be made more explicit through affective encounters that the chapter materializes. A cat's cradle performs Haraway's figurations in order to play in the naturecultures of Lego and human children and clarify how 'diverse bodies and meanings co-shape one another' (Haraway, 2008: 4). The aim is to take up familiar discourses and stretch them by considering the enactment and generative potential that material-discursive entanglements, events and encounters offer to conceptualizations of gender in early childhood.

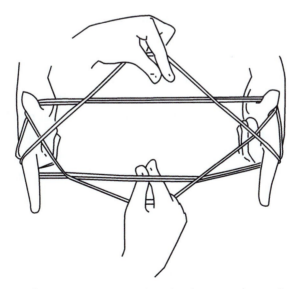

Figure 5.1 String figuring. Source: Jayne (1906) at http://www.stringfigures.info/cfj/real-cats-cradle.html

String figuring Lego involves processes of grappling with ideas about gender in early childhood that ignites a set of difficult questions: *What is Lego?* A plastic chemical compound? Made entirely by robots? *What is Lego for?* A learning resource? For pleasure and play? A collectable artefact? An aide to cognitive development? *Whom is Lego for?* Children? Adults? Animals? Sea creatures? Microbes and germs? The wealthy? The able-bodied? The dextrous? *What does Lego represent?* Simplicity? Denmark? Profitable capitalist enterprise? Gender neutrality? Gender stereotypes? Construction toy history? Response to and shaper of popular culture? *What does Lego do? What* else *does Lego do?* Pollution? Artwork? Conservation? *What do we do with what Lego does?* There are no simple answers to these questions but asking them highlights the tangles, the knots, the deeply enmeshed and interwoven stories that are available, that are joyful, hopeful, distressing, desperate and troubling. This chapter does not aim to arrive at a neat set of conclusions about gender in early childhood via an experiment with Lego. Rather the goal is to get at complexity and multiplicity and so to offer an illustration of the affordances of deep thoughtfulness and to underscore how the knowledges that get produced today are indebted to the past and future.

In order to articulate this game of cat's cradle necessitates that strings are pulled from developmental psychology, neuroscience, early childhood pedagogy, commodity culture, scientific manufacturing, as well as my own biographical and embodied encounters with Lego. I rummage around to assemble these strings as tangles and knots which facilitate 'effective critical practice' (Haraway, 1994: 69) to think both more intensively and expansively about gender as processes of becoming in early childhood.

Haraway (1992) offers feminist figuration as reconfiguration – a call to feminists to 'resist representation, resist literal figuration and erupt in powerful new tropes, new figures of speech, new turns of historical possibility' (p. 86). Haraway's figurations materialize from assembling, arranging and rearranging processes, convictions, bodies, herstories and languages. They are not (only) metaphorical but reveal the diverse political and moral dynamics embedded within them:

> Haraway challenges us to open ourselves up to the metaphors and figures she uses and to the complexity of her vision, even as their links to more familiar theories and concepts are not always at first apparent. Haraway is an advocate of multiple and cross-cutting literacies, which she believes are essential both for reading the complex and global issues of society today and in the future. (Schneider, 2005: 22)

Bates (2015) argues that figurations not only reveal underlying assumptions, failures and contradictions but also hold the potential to expose the emergent effects of such discourses; that is, specific orientations are formed from the convergence of multiple discourses that are not possible on their own. Hence, revisiting and renewing these discourses enable their various combined effects to be understood and reimagined. This chapter attempts to revisit and renew discourses about the relationship between Lego and gender.

The string game of cat's cradle provides a seriously playful and playfully serious foraging method. It maps the processes, discourses, matter and bodies that form a figuration, attending to both the significant and playful and tracing the material affects. Haraway weaves her cradle 'not just to read the webs of knowledge production but to reconfigure what counts as knowledge in the interests of reconstituting the generative forces of embodiment' (1994: 62). The string of a cat's cradle is both metaphor and matter; the game can only be played through bodily action and is therefore a dynamic map that cannot trace a single lineage. Each cat's cradle figure contains the same ingredients but materializes differently; each knot is a figuration in itself, and they can be arranged and rearranged to reconfigure what counts as knowledge about entanglements (Haraway, 1994: 62). Each figure is formed from another and is an immanent state of becoming.

> Cyborgs and companion species each bring together the human and non-human, the organic and technological, carbon and silicon, freedom and structure, history and myth, the rich and the poor, the state and the subject, diversity and depletion, modernity and postmodernity, and nature and culture in unexpected ways. (Haraway, 2003: 4)

Leg godt!

LEGO® is made from **ABS**
(**acrylonitrile butadiene styrene**),
a **thermoplastic polymer** comprised of three **monomers**.
The first monomer,
acrylonitrile, gives the bricks strength.
The second,
1,3-butadiene, gives them resilience (i.e. stops them from snapping so easily)
and the third,
styrene, gives them a shiny, hard surface.

Mixed with **colorants** then **polymerised** (hardened) with the help of an initiator:
potassium peroxydisulphate.
LEGO® buys pre-made ABS granules and
injects them into brick shapes on a massive scale.
LEGO® make **20 billion bricks each year**
(35,000 bricks a minute)
The Guinness Book of World Record claims
LEGO produces more plastic tyres
than anyone else.

(Kennedy, 2014)

Lego in early childhood

Lego bricks, but perhaps more typically the bigger Duplo bricks, are a common feature in early childhood. Lego has been and continues to be ubiquitous; it is everywhere and it matters. Lego is perhaps the most widely available and engaged form of block play for children and adults alike. As reported in *The Daily Telegraph* (2017) recently:

> Lego is the world's number three toymaker in the £70billion a year global market and the leading industry player in $15bn European market, according to data from analysts. It has consistently seen off competition from challengers, delivering near-constant double-digit growth for a decade, with the Billund-based business adding increasingly technical products to its traditional building sets and mini-figures, as well as video games and franchise such as the Lego films. Grown-ups – known as AFoLs, or Adult Fans of Lego – have also been targeted with high-end products, and the company has also introduced a range targeted at females as it looked to tackle intense competition.

Block play has long been hailed an effective pedagogy in early childhood education claimed to support brain growth and fine motor skills (Drew et al., 2003a, 2008; Geist, 2009; Wolfgang et al., 2001). Building with blocks is argued to provide one of the most valuable learning experiences available to young children. Playing with blocks stimulates learning in all domains of development: intellectual, physical, social-emotional and language. Wolfgang et al. (2001) claim that block play is fundamental for later cognitive success in learning maths and numbers. Block play in early childhood has typically been understood through developmental psychology discourses which rest on an understanding of natural progression through ages and stages of early childhood development (Burman, 2008). For example, under threes are understood to explore and experiment with blocks to develop fine motor skills, colour recognition, cause and effect, and mathematical concepts such as matching and size (Geist, 2009).

> Sometimes I find it challenging being colour-blind; it can be very difficult to distinguish colours and I have no idea if they clash or not. Also, only having a student budget ... I frequently have to make compromises with the size and colour of models, which is why there is a lot of grey in them! (Barney Main, 18, UK in Lipkowitz, 2011: 38)

The social benefits noted for children under three years of age include self-confidence and expressive language. From three years onwards, it is claimed that children play with blocks in a more sophisticated way as they engage in pretend play, and so the construction of built enclosures (zoos, farms, castles) is commonly identified. By four and five, children's block play is more proficient and coordinated, with the construction of more complex buildings and greater social engagement with peers in the form or imaginary/pretend play. Drew et al. (2008) claim that block play shows the opportunity for conceptual understanding in structural engineering as children explore forces of gravity, compression, tension and the relationship between materials and successful design to achieve balance, stability and even aesthetic sensibility. Science is also being learnt through block play as children make predictions, comparisons and experiment with cause and effect, stability and balance.

> I think it's important to just play with putting bricks together, not even building anything: two little pieces you put together can suddenly look a bit like something you've seen elsewhere. (Deborah Higdon, Canada, 52 in Lipkowitz, 2011: 70)

There is clear guidance available to early years teachers (e.g. ECERS-R, see Harms et al., 2003a, 2003b) about the type of environment and the materials that are necessary to encourage block play. The texture and material is significant with encouragement to include cardboard, wooden, foam and plastic blocks of differing sizes to meet the needs of children at different ages and stages of development. The adult teacher role is also important. Drew et al. (2008) stress that teachers will benefit from professional development that emphasizes their own active enquiry and creative exploration with materials to best facilitate children's engagement with block play. By asking reasoning questions such as 'which row is bigger?' 'how many blocks in that structure?' teachers can actively support child development and learning.

This account makes clear that the evidence about the value of block play in early childhood education is squarely framed by developmental psychology discourses. As children pass through normative stages of development, there is scientific evidence that playing with blocks can aide brain growth (Newman et al., 2016). What is notable from a feminist new materialist standpoint though is that blocks, Lego or otherwise, are viewed in largely apolitical terms. Blocks are regarded as inanimate objects to be manipulated by humans for human development. The humble block is an object to be organized by adults as means to scaffold children's educational development. Despite a very long tradition of blocks and bricks in early childhood, dating back to Froebel and Montessori which have very distinct philosophical underpinnings, the block nevertheless retains a status as *inanimate* object that exists solely to facilitate child development. Following Bennett's (2010) ideas about the vibrancy of matter invites alternative ways in which to engage with the block. Viewing and sensing the block in other ways require that the feminist researcher resists the overwhelming temptation to anthropomorphize play scenarios so that the human is always central to investigations. Rather than beginning from the premise that it is people who animate docile objects, might it be possible to wonder how objects can function differently? What happens if blocks are viewed as lively objects that act on people in unanticipated ways? Or as Bennett articulates about the liveliness of objects and the vibrancy of matter:

> Is that which, by virtue of its particular location in an assemblage and the fortuity of being in the right place at the right time, makes the difference, makes things happen, becomes the decisive force catalyzing an event. (Bennett, 2010: 9)

As Macrae (2012) stresses, we need to be attuned to the productive way that an object resurfaces and to the effects of its reappearance which becomes significant. In early childhood contexts, framed by child-centred pedagogies, decentring the human is an impossibly difficult task. But in attempting to do so, a set of interesting questions and lines of enquiry are opened up. Working with diffractive methodologies to study blocks in early childhood contexts might present surprising and productive possibilities to engage with the idea that gender is produced, emergent and generated through the intra- and inter-actions within play assemblages, where the block is a significant and lively participant. If agency is understood as confederate and distributed beyond the individual human subject, it then becomes possible to start to re-conceptualize 'how we come to think and act in particular ways, and how creative evolution takes place through those actions' (Davies, 2010: 56).

Feminist post-structuralist accounts of the trouble with block play

I want to retrace ideas about block play in early childhood to feminist research conducted in the 1990s since it offers other important ruptures to the 'evidence-based', taken-for-granted, anthropocentric, gender-neutral messages about the value of block play in early childhood that tend to circulate, and which have been outlined so far in this chapter. Twenty years ago, in a chapter entitled 'Girls don't do bricks: Gender and sexuality in the primary classroom', Epstein (1998[1995]) reported on her encounters with block play and the troubling gendered patterns of play that she identified through research with a group of young children. She theorized gendered play in childhood through Butler's concepts of the heterosexual matrix, heteronormativity and compulsory heterosexuality. The account of the gendered and heterosexist behaviour identified made an important contribution to debates about the significance of gender, race, class and other inequalities that routinely play out in primary schools and nursery classrooms but tended not to feature within mainstream educational research at the time. Within Epstein's account, blocks continue to be presented as inanimate objects manipulated by humans, but the crucial distinction in her work was the recognition that objects are imbued with discursive and representational meaning. Through her study, she identified the worrying means by which boys dominate classroom space through the organization of blocks in particular ways and the masculine structures that are built by boys in those spaces that then act to exclude girls. By creating space and opportunities for girls to play with blocks (in girl-only groups), she found that not only did they become deeply engrossed in the activity but they were also immersed in the discursive and material gendered practices of building. Her chapter stressed the need for teachers to actively orchestrate and choreograph the learning space and materials to mitigate gendered patterns of play:

> What is needed in the introduction of activities and organisation of the classroom in such a way that alternative and oppositional discourses and discursive practices are available to children. (p. 67)

The girls constructed a Princess Palace, which Epstein argued positioned block play within competing discourses that both challenge *and* reinscribe ideas about gender in childhood. The human intentionality (of the feminist teacher) and the agency that children were able to exercise to resist heterosexist play rested upon a view of the classroom as a space that could be manipulated and reconfigured (by adult humans) to produce other possibilities:

> The key here is in creating and providing classroom materials and curriculum content which both necessitate activities which run contrary to heterosexist gendered stereotypes *and* which allow children to remain comfortable in their play with their current (but developing) understandings of what it might mean to be a boy or a girl. (p. 68)

A few years later, Mindy Blaise (2005b) identified the persistence of similar gendered patterns in block play, with boys dominating space and girls routinely denied the same play opportunities, in kindergarten. Blaise extended Epstein's work to question how gender in early childhood is socially, culturally, historically and politically constructed. Central to her argument was the notion that gender resides in contexts and cannot simply be understood as located in the individual human subject. Blaise contributed to debates about gender in childhood by arguing that it is an embodied performance, materialized through dress, bodily expressions and play. She stressed that gender must be understood as produced through discursive *and* material practices. Epstein and Blaise were among a growing body of feminist scholars (Arnot & Weiner, 1987; Davies, 1989, Francis, 1998; Walkerdine, 1981) throughout the late 1980s and into the early 2000s to argue that children exercise agency to consciously and unconsciously perform/construct gendered subjectivities, and crucially children find ways to resist heteronormative positioning within discourses. This was ground-breaking research of the time that fundamentally challenged dominant ideas about children, childhood, gender and sexualities.

Robinson and Jones-Diaz (2016) recently noted that feminist accounts of gender in early childhood continue to predominantly focus on discursive practices. The emergent shift to new materialist approaches was considered important in its attempt to

> rectify an imbalance between discursive and material ways of knowing and experiencing the world, arguing that discourse alone does not allow for a full understanding of how subjects become who they are and know the world ... In the context of understanding gender in childhood, these perspectives highlight the importance of exploring how the material (e.g. bodies, buildings, outdoor spaces, sounds, trees, toys and other objects) affects the ways of knowing and becoming gendered. Through an analysis of the complexity of active and constitutive relationships or entanglements that exist between the material, discourse and affect, and how gender is mobilised in these spaces that are continually being re-constructed, different experiences of gender can be explored. (p. 196)

Pulling at these various strings in this game of cat's cradle offers multiple conceptualizations and accounts of block play in early childhood contexts. Furthermore, it becomes possible to discern overlapping matters of concern and philosophical patterns of engagement. The significance of context, space, place and the material composition of block play re-emerges within these various accounts from developmental psychology, neuroscience, feminist post-strucuturalism and new materialism. Spatially, the designation and organization of specific zones for early childhood pedagogies both create and shut down possibilities for the ways that gender manifests through play. As argued by Pacini-Ketchabaw (2012), temporality is also significant in early childhood. She refers to commonplace 'clocking practices' in early childhood settings which act to regulate and shape how children can play and make sense of themselves, but they also present other productive possibilities when new materialist-inspired questions are asked. In addition to asking what clocking practices represent, attention to the material-discursive affordances invites a different set of questions, such as:

> What kinds of work does the clock do? What role do humans play in operating and producing clocking practices? What role does the clock play in producing early childhood practices and in reconfiguring human-clock boundaries and relations? What sort of temporalities do different clocking practices engender? What sort of shifts in assemblages do different clocks and different clocking practices encourage? How are specific practices of early childhood education mediated by various clocks and clocking practices? Do different clocks in different spaces do different work and engender different bodies and bodily practices and relations? (2012: 159)

These sorts of questions can similarly be asked of blocks and block play to extend feminist enquiries into how gender is materially and discursively produced in early childhood contexts. Feminist new materialism is concerned to question where, how and when blocks come to matter and invite curiosity into what gets produced in terms of the material-discursive generation of gender. Taking a step back 'to make the familiar strange' (Osgood, 2014) and challenge habitual ways of thinking and being in early childhood contexts allows blocks to be observed, sensed and encountered as agentic. A concern with the humble block reaches beyond what it is, as material object, to its performative aspects (i.e. what the block can do and what it functions together within a given context, at a particular time, and in relation to the bodies it encounters and their vitalities).

> You can be working close up on a model and it seems alright, but when you stand back it's not quite right or you have missed some detail that could look

better. The only thing to do is take some of the model apart and rebuild it. You always feel better in the end, even if it takes longer. (Duncan Titmarsh, 40, UK in Lipkowitz, 2011: 165)

Engaging with blocks, as situated entanglements, involves considering how blocks, children and educators emerge within practices. What kinds of subjectivities are afforded, what kinds of actions are afforded and what kinds of actions are excluded (Barad, 2007). Block play can be rethought of as intra-active practices that are embedded within, and generate, a multitude of dynamic networks. The challenge is both to understand the ways in which blocks are embedded in early childhood practices and to consider how they generate affects. Decades of feminist research presents multiple ways in which children and educators experiment with block practices in attempts to find ways to engage with the block, and for the block to engage them, differently. Becoming with blocks, being open to what might emerge, involves an openness to reimagining how we think about, sense and act with blocks. Focusing on the block as a material-discursive element in early childhood block play requires attending to the interweaving of the block with other bodies, as well as what emerges. The block and its relational entanglement with other bodies (human and non-human) are vital for subjectivities to emerge.

Der var engang: Storying Lego

It takes a lot of patience and determination to rebuild, but it will always be worth it in the end. Often it turns out better than the original! (Deborah Higdon, Canada, 52 in Lipkowitz, 2011: 68)

A Danish carpenter, Ole Kirk Christiansen, began making wooden toys in the 1930s in the small town of Billund, which according to Siren (2013) remains a modest form of capitalism with one-storey buildings nestled along wide streets, dotted with trees. Aside from the airport and amusement park, there is very little to denote the lucrative global success of the Lego company for which the town is infamous.

As the success of the toys grew, they were branded 'Lego', a word derived from the Danish phrase *leg godt*, meaning 'to play well'. By the mid-1940s, Lego expanded to produce plastic toys, among them an early version of the now familiar interlocking bricks, calling them 'Automatic Binding Bricks'. The bricks, originally manufactured from cellulose acetate were a development of the traditional stackable wooden blocks of the time. By 1951, plastic toys accounted for half of the Lego company's output.

> Latin (verb) *Lego* means:
> 1. furl (sail), weigh (anchor)
> 2. gather, collect (cremated bones)
> 3. pick out
> 4. read
>
> (Source: http://www.latin-dictionary.net/definition/25465/
> lego-legere-legi-lectus)

By 1954, Christiansen's son, Godtfred, had taken on the role of managing director at Lego and identified the potential for Lego bricks to become a system for creative play. The modern brick design was developed; however, it took another five years to find the right material for it, ABS (acrylonitrile butadiene styrene) polymer. The modern Lego brick design was patented in 1958. The Lego Group's Duplo product line was introduced in 1969 and offered a range of simple blocks measuring twice the width, height and depth of standard Lego blocks and aimed at younger children.

> I was 18 months old when I got my first Lego Duplo set, but moved on to LEGO sets shortly afterwards – and I haven't stopped since then! (Barney Main, 18, UK in Lipkowitz, 2011: 36)

As the decades have passed, Lego has been the subject of both celebration and criticism by feminists, environmentalists, parents and children for what Lego is, what it represents and what it does. Some of these threads will be picked up and the knots and tangles attended to in the remainder of this chapter

Everything is Awesome! Plastic pollution

> During 2015, the total CO2 emissions for the production and distribution of Lego bricks was 1,138,187 tonnes. This is equivalent to approximately 22 grams of CO2 per 2x4 Lego brick, when considering *a brick's full life*. (The Lego Group, 2016: 39, my emphasis)

In 2016, The Lego Group published an eighty-page *Responsibility Report*, setting out its activities and key social, environmental and economic impacts, and the risks and opportunities related to its business operations. As an increasingly globalized company, the report outlines the measures it has taken to address the environmental impact of producing millions upon millions of plastic blocks each year. The environmental initiatives are multiple but include off-shore wind farms across Europe and solar panels (equivalent to five football pitches) upon the roof of its factory in Jiaxing, China, where a large proportion of the 19,000 strong global workforce is located.

For all its affordances Lego presents feminists, environmentalists and environmental feminists with much to be agitated by: the constellation of carbon footprint, incitement to disposability, endless production, and increasing commercialization and commodification are troubling. But might it be possible to take up Haraway's invitation to stay with the trouble? Bennett (2010) argues that 'commodification is not in full control of the effects of the encounter between human bodies and commercial artifacts' (p. 32) and goes on to stress that something can 'temporarily jar humans out of the stupor of their duly sequential representing and recognizing' (p. 53). The environmental implications of the production, circulation and acquisition of Lego are complex, and it requires that agency is understood as distributed and not solely the province of humans. Lego is not an inanimate object; it is lively matter that produces and generates within webs of affective forces, through multiple situations and events. The material formations in which Lego bricks and figures participate can reveal implications for vital materialism (Bennett, 2010) and broaden our sense of care in relation to the world of human, non-human and things. The consumption and disposal of Lego is a lively matter: 'The sheer volume of commodities and the hyperconsumptive necessity of junking them to make room for new ones, conceals the vitality of matter' (Bennett, 2010: 5). Lego is endlessly reproduced, is endlessly discarded and endlessly lives on in unexpected ecologies. One powerful example is the ongoing liveliness of Lego in the aftermath of a spillage over twenty years ago. In 1997, a container ship, the *Tokio Express*, was hit by a giant wave, which tilted the ship violently from side to side; in the process sixty-two containers plunged into the sea 20 miles from the Cornish coast in southwest England:

> Nearly five million pieces of Lego in one day is obviously a significant amount but so much debris washes up all the time – the Lego is but a drop in the ocean! Although the Lego used to wash up intact it's gradually breaking down into smaller and smaller pieces. Maybe it will eventually be unrecognisable. Micro plastic pollution is a huge issue. (Gailor, 2016: 36)

Vital materiality can never really be discarded or disposed of; it continues its activities even as unwanted or lost commodity. Bennett (2010) writes of 'thing-power' as the curious ability of inanimate things to animate, to act, to produce dramatic and subtle effects. As outlined in Chapter 2, feminist new materialism refuses a singular emphasis upon texts, linguistics and discursive accounts and instead argues for discursive practices to be connected to material phenomena (Alaimo & Hekman, 2008; Barad, 2007) through plastic readings. Bringing discourse and materiality into play with each other enables a move away from creating a false dichotomy between description and reality 'to matters of practices, doings, and actions' (Barad, 2007: 135). Embracing plasticity as a concept and way of enacting investigations creates a 'theoretical perspective that does not privilege either language or reality but instead explains and builds on their intimate interaction' (Hekman, 2010: 3). The liveliness of the Lego brick, how it is framed discursively and what it produces materially insist upon a material-discursive reading:

> We've had quite a few reports from the Netherlands – the Lego has been washing up there for years. A beachcomber in Texas recently found a Lego octopus and someone else in Maine, USA found one of the Lego life rafts. A beachgoer in Australia found a blue Lego flipper and we've spotted Lego spear guns in montages of beach finds posted online by beachcombers in California. In recent weeks we've also had reports from Portugal and France. Obviously it's hard to tell from a single find whether it's from the *Tokio Express* or just a random loss but oceanographers believe that Lego will have travelled all around the world by now. We tend to look at patterns, i.e. whether or not more than one item has washed up and if so whether they are pieces we recognize. (Gailor, 2016: 38)

Another knot: Dispatchwork

Walking down a street, in central London, with my children. We are on our way to the British Museum; the sun is shining; we are lost in conversation. At once we are collectively hailed, captivated by something otherworldly, bright, arresting, provocative: tiny Lego bricks, forming a temporary, structural tapestry of repair to a nineteenth-century wall. Jan Vormann, a German artist, has been entangled with a lesser-known form of Lego globalization over the past decade. Through the project, Dispatchwork, Lego and Vormann have travelled the globe to offer an investigation into the vital materiality of Lego as it is produced and as it generates alternative stories in multiple contexts.

The Lego as-street-art installation interrupts, recuperates, provokes and heals crumbling walls, pillars and churches and offers a gentle provocation

Image 5.2 Dispatchwork, London. Source: http://www.theguardian.com/
artanddesign/gallery/2008/nov/14/design

to pay attention to matter – and how matter is entangled, productive and
agentic. Artistic interventions of this nature are uniquely placed to undertake
important work to extend and challenge entrenched discourses. The hegemonic
discourses that provide explanations about what Lego makes possible and what

it symbolizes have been traced throughout this chapter. However, through its doings dispatchwork is able to disrupt and stretch discursive accounts through materialized figuration. The out-of-place Lego brick invites questions about environmental challenges and provokes thoughts about how we might produce more live-able worlds. Eco-art projects such as this illustrate that using creative engagement through the arts might provoke shifts in values, beliefs, attitudes and habits and generate community involvement and provide alternative modes of consumption. The project has inspired others to engage in this practice, which has expanded the global reach of the art installation. An interactive map (https:// dispatchwork.jimdo.com) traces the propagation of this artistic practice and the affective flows that the humble Lego brick is producing on a global scale.

Serious play: Playfully serious

Haraway (2008: 235) stresses that:

> Inquiry becomes inextricably rich and detailed in the flesh of complexity and nonlinear difference and its required semiotic figures. Encounters among human beings and other animals change in this web. Not least people can stop looking for some single defining difference between them and everybody else and understand that they are in rich and largely uncharted, material-semiotic, flesh to flesh, face to face connection with a host of significant others.

This chapter has attempted to get at some of the richness, detail and complexity that are presented when Lego is taken seriously. By following unanticipated and surprising lines of enquiry, the storying of Lego and its active part in producing gender in early childhood has taken multiple, interwoven and complex directions. I want to momentarily bring the adventure back to a concern with anthropocentric notions of what Lego can do for us in the sense of human cognitive development. In January 2016, I was invited to participate in a Playing Seriously with Lego Workshop. I was intrigued; as a mother of young children, I frequently find myself engaged in Lego construction but not so much with the imaginative play that is more open-ended and fantastical; in fact I am routinely excluded from this form of play at home, which tends to take place behind closed bedroom doors as my children enter into otherworldly spaces of espionage and danger (Osgood, 2015a).

> I was about 7 when I was first introduced to LEGO bricks. I stopped building, like many kids do, but I started again as an adult ... Then I found the online LEGO

community, joined a local club for adults, and started to display publicly and post my work on the internet. (Sebastian Arts, 27, Netherlands in Lipkowitz, 2011: 133)

The *Lego Serious Play Method*, according to Blair and Rillo (2016), and earlier Burgi et al. (2005), is intended for adult employees to work with metaphor and Lego to share knowledge, problem-solve and make decisions. Within a workshop scenario, a facilitator (trained in the method) guides the participants through a series of questions, about a given issue or problem currently encountered by the employees. The workshop I attended was concerned to explore the persistence of gender inequalities in higher education. We were invited to build 3D Lego models that represented our current experiences of working in higher education; specifically we were advised to construct our 'professional identity'.

The method requires that participants utilize visual, auditory and kinaesthetic skills, and furthermore, insists that all participants are given a voice (through the creation and explanation of the representational model). It is not my intention to dwell upon the workshop, the models that were created or the discussions that ensued. Unsurprisingly though a range of familiar discourses were generated about the marginalization, oppression and everyday sexism that persists within Higher Education Institutions (HEIs), especially for working-mothers and LGBTQI+ academics (Osgood et al., 2016). Of greater interest within the discussion unfolding in this chapter though is the learning theory that underpins the method and possibilities to reconfigure the method and consider its productive potential for future feminist new materialist investigations.

Image 5.3 My professional identity. Source: Author's own image, January 2016

Burgi & Roos (2003) stress that within the method, play is defined as a limited, structured and voluntary activity that involves the imaginary. It is a temporally and spatially contained event, structured by rules, conventions and agreements among the players, uncoerced by authority figures, and drawing on elements of fantasy and creative imagination. It is broadly based upon Piagetian constructivist theories of learning, which promote the idea that effective learning occurs when people are engaged in constructing a product, something external to themselves. Imagination is a core element, defined through the method as the means to describe something, to create something and to challenge something. Lego Serious Play concerns the interplay between these three kinds of imagination that make up strategic imagination. It is evident from this account of the method that it sits in stark contrast to feminist new materialist methodologies that are shaped by uncertainty and that do not intentionally evolve in temporal order but are more typically ongoing processes that are lived and take place in everyday action and practice. Feminist new materialist approaches tend towards an emergent, (k)not-knowingness (Osgood, 2018) that attends to the messy, embodied and affective entanglements as they are produced through micro-moments (Moxnes & Osgood, 2018). A feminist new materialist workshop would take a very different form and commence with much less clear intentionality and outcome-driven objectives. It raises interesting questions about creativity, learning, social processes and the potential of Lego to produce new knowledge. While the workshop I attended was framed by a concern to generate new knowledge about gender in higher education among a specific group of employees, and the process was both enjoyable and productive, the outcomes were very predictable – reflecting back that which we already knew. I wonder what else a Lego Serious Play workshop, one framed by feminist new materialism and where the humble Lego brick is encountered as agentic and lively, might produce.

Re-turns and dis/continuities: What does Lego do? What do we with what it does?

In Latin, *Lego* has various definitions, one of which is 'to assemble'. Throughout this chapter, Lego has been productive; it has been an affective force that has generated, assembled, other ideas about gender in early childhood. Tracing the threads and staying with the trouble within the knots encountered have proved generative but inconclusive. I have not arrived at a recognizable or contained approach to investigating gender. This practice though of creating patterns and knots has, according to Haraway (1994: 64):

> result(ed) in some serious surprises … Cat's cradle invites a sense of collective work, of one person not being able to make all the patterns alone. One does not 'win' at cat's cradle; the goal is more interesting and more open-ended than that. It is not always possible to repeat interesting patterns, and figuring out what happened to result in intriguing patterns is an embodied analytical skill …[it] is a game about complex, collaborative practices for making and passing on culturally interesting patterns.

This chapter has responded to Haraway's insistence that we need to engage in wayfaring practices and indulge in 'off the beaten path' methods in order to get at other ways to encounter the world of which we form part. The Lego company proclaim that it is their intention that children should build creations from their imaginations through processes of self-discovery to pursue a 'world without limits'. Following string figures through a game of cat's cradle, this chapter has pursued a project of staying with the trouble presented in knots and tangles. It has deliberately avoided a chronological and linear account; instead it offers a transversal mapping that seeks to capture the multilayered, entangled, emergent, re-turning through the archives of feminist thought and following lines to other frayed strings. Lego does important work for engaging with ideas and practices about how gender is produced through early childhood assemblages. It works on multiple plains to nudge habitual thought elsewhere. My aim has been to excavate, trouble, challenge, grapple and extend ideas about Lego so that debates about childhood and gender can recognize the complexity of productive processes. The girl child, the boy child, the teacher, the parent, media, toys, classrooms and playgrounds are all active in these processes. So while discursive accounts about what Lego, and block play more generally, does to gendered possibilities, there is value in attending to material-discursive possibilities if we are prepared to be open to the not-known, not-yet-known and (k)not-known. Charlotte Benjamin, aged seven, raises valid concerns in her letter to Lego which caught worldwide media attention (via Twitter):

Dear Lego company,

My name is Charlotte. I am 7 years old and
I love Lego but I don't like
that there are more Lego boy people
and barely any Lego girls.

Today I went to a store and saw Lego in two sections
the girls pink
and
the boys blue.
All the girls did was sit at home, go to the beach, and shop, and they had no jobs
but
the boys went on adventures, worked, saved people, and had jobs, even swam
with sharks.
I want you to make more Lego girl people and let them go on adventures and
have fun ok!?!
Thank you.
From Charlotte

The feminist research into how gender is regulated and produced in early childhood contexts, outlined in this chapter, stresses that Charlotte has agency. Indeed, she has exercised that agency in her public criticism of Lego for its heterosexist toy design and promotion. On a more domestic level, she can also exercise agency in what Lego she chooses and how she plays with it. Following Epstein (1998), Blaise (2005b) and Robinson (2005), McKnight 2015, Charlotte should be actively supported in childhood contexts (through the organization of classroom space, place, objects, learning materials, toys and curriculum objectives) and through parenting practices at home that are attuned to challenging heteronormative discourses by resisting stereotypically gendered clothes and toys. What I have endeavoured to pursue in this chapter though is that Lego can be thought about as imbued with thing-power, carrying and transmitting traces of other assemblages within and stemming from a Lego assemblage that opens up ideas about how gender is more than a human concern. How gender is produced in early childhood is complex and made up of physical flows, languages, gendered discourses, visceral feelings and cultural practices. Taking the liveliness of matter, asking what Lego does and what we might do with what it does offers a multilayered, speculative account that opens up endless possibilities. I have 'rummaged around looking for the parts', with which to tell these stories, although through the rummaging parts also found me. These stories are comprised of entangled knots, patterns and string figures; they are troubling and hopeful stories, and they are speculative fabulation. Through processes of scavenging, foraging and wayfaring, the generation of this chapter has involved tentacular processes of sensing, feeling and making connections of possibility to connect complex stories that relate to each other (Haraway, 2016: 2) and offer other ways in which to encounter ideas and practices in early childhood contexts.

6

Enacting Feminist Materialist Movement Pedagogies in the Early Years

Mindy Blaise and Veronica Pacini-Ketchabaw

Photograph 6.1 Moving bodies. Author's photograph

Introduction

It has been well established that a developmental and binary logic characterizes early childhood education, rendering it highly problematic (Blaise, 2005a, 2013b). One of the concerns that feminist scholars working in early childhood education have regarding this oppositional logic is how it simultaneously reinforces gender norms and gender stereotypes, while also constructing a gender-neutral child (Blaise, 2005, 2013b; MacNaughton, 2000). The purpose of this chapter is to establish how feminist materialist movement pedagogies are part of a gender politics, how they unsettle foundational and developmental thinking, and what they offer the field of early childhood education. We begin by showing how three shifts within theory (developmental, feminist post-structural, feminist materialist) change pedagogies by attending to gender differently. Data generated from a movement inquiry that took place in an early childhood centre in Canada is then used to illuminate how feminist materialist theories can be enacted in practice (which we call feminist movement pedagogies). It is important to note that the aim of the movement inquiry was not to support children's development, although their development was indeed supported. Instead, the movement inquiry set out to reconfigure how we think about moving bodies. As such, these feminist movement pedagogies do more than just reconfiguring bodies; they also *activate new political thought.* This is a shift away from simply being concerned with supporting a child's linear growth and development, towards rethinking movement itself.

As feminist movement pedagogies, gender and gender power relations are significant to understanding how movements produce bodies (Manning, 2014) and, specifically, how movements produce child gendered bodies. Feminist movement pedagogies are transversal, occurring in moments where we (educators and researchers) feel entangled and are aware of how our human bodies are 'shift[ing] and mov[ing] with/in environments, not as individuals, but as collective assemblages of human and nonhuman, material and immaterial sensations' (Barry, 2016: 2). This kind of transversality shifts the focus from the moving individual child body to a more expansive or collective way of understanding movements and bodies. In doing so, it also challenges us to move away from always understanding motor development in a linear direction. Instead, it pushes us to think about how feminist materialist movement pedagogies activate gendered and more-than-human bodies and what they can potentially *do* across all sorts of bodies. Before illustrating various feminist materialist movement pedagogies, we briefly outline three theoretical and pedagogical shifts.

Developmental movement pedagogies

Although there are several theoretical models of development (i.e. psychoanalytic, psychosocial, environmental, cognitive development) that influence motor development, Arnold Gesell's (1880–1961) maturational theory has played a significant role in the expansion of child development. Maturation drives this perspective and assumes that developmental stage sequences are wired into a child's genes and that these stages unfold according to an inner timetable. The process of maturation recognizes that a child is a product of her environment and development is directed from within (Crain, 2011). From this view, development always unfolds in fixed, directional and discrete sequences, which is controlled by the genetic blueprint. In other words, maturation has been naturalized (Burman, 1994), solidifying and separating the nature–culture divide. Sequential development continues after birth and throughout the lifespan. Over time, a child's motor development gradually becomes more advanced and organized. Although children will vary in their rates of development, a maturational perspective assumes they all proceed through the same, predictable sequences. For example, the development of rudimentary locomotor abilities, such as horizontal movements, is presented in a sequence of abilities matched up with an approximate age of onset (see Table 6.1). These abilities move from simply scooting one's body across a surface to walking on all fours. Eventually this will lead to standing upright and moving independently on two feet.

Gesell believed that it was important to understand the sequences of development and that there was fluctuation within this order. Pedagogically, teachers should not force children to learn in ways that run counter to their nature. Child body movements such as reflexes, reaching, grasping, releasing, pulling up, walking, climbing, throwing and pinching are directional and discrete. From this perspective, it is important not to push the child until she is ready. Instead, teachers must modify their developmental movement pedagogies to the individual child's state of readiness and special abilities. This view zooms in on an individual child and assumes that we already know what a body can do. In addition, having an ages and stages framework only reinforces this notion of

Table 6.1 Horizontal child body movements

Selected abilities	Approximate age of onset
Scooting	Third month
Crawling	Sixth month
Creeping	Ninth month
Walking on all fours	Eleventh month

(Gallahue et al., 2012: 143)

knowing and certainty because it links a body movement with an approximate age. These traditional developmental movement theories and pedagogies are creating a child body that either can do particular movements (or not), and at the same time they are disciplining the body, guiding the body, moulding the body, and creating gendered girl and boy child bodies.

A teacher working from a developmental perspective would tend to focus on the muscular aspects of movement by considering gross and fine motor skills, commonly planning different activities for these areas of motor development. Stress would usually be placed on developing a variety of fundamental locomotor, manipulative and stability activities progressing from the simple to the complex as the child becomes 'ready'. For example, gross motor skill development might be supported by encouraging children to step up onto and walk along a concrete wall outside (see Photograph 6.1). Depending on their stage of development, a child might need the assistance of a teacher to hold their hand, or they might be able to balance themselves and walk independently. Fine motor skills, on the other hand, are usually developed through writing, typing and painting, and these activities traditionally happen indoors.

It is almost impossible to think outside of this binary logic when developmental movement pedagogies rely on various hyper-separations such as indoor/outdoor activities, quiet/loud actions and fine/gross muscular aspects of movement. Gendered girl and boy bodies are created through these taken-for-granted fine and gross motor activities. For example, girls are often expected and encouraged to develop fine motor skills when they are asked to quietly spend time with their friends drawing pictures or making books at the writing centre. Boys, on the other hand, are expected to be rambunctious and are often quickly encouraged to move their loud and out-of-control bodies outside so as not to disturb the quieter indoor activities. Classrooms, for example, are designed to meet these expectations when we set up the outdoor yard for big body moving games and for shouting and yelling, whereas the indoor area is created for quiet reading or working with still, silent and docile child bodies.

Feminist post-structural movement pedagogies

In the 1990s, early childhood gender scholars turned to post-structural theories about knowledge, truth and power to understand the discursive construction of gender identities and gender power relations. Work initiated by Valerie Walkerdine (1981), Bronwyn Davies ([1989] 2003) and Barrie Thorne (1993) led the way by contesting developmental and socialization theories of children's gender construction. Their research argued that gender was a socially, culturally and historically shifting construct. An important contribution that came from this research was a new awareness of children's agency and the role that children themselves play in constructing gender, including how children take part in both challenging and reinforcing gender binaries, gender stereotypes and gender norms. The concept of gender performativity is also significant because it suggests that gender is a kind of performance or way of 'acting out' gender (Butler, 1994). From this perspective, gender is performed through the ways we talk about ourselves as girls and women or boys and men and by specific bodily practices or movements – and their repetitions. Repeatedly performing gender according to traditional gender roles and gender stereotypes, such as unruly boys' bodies vs subdued girls' bodies, makes us believe that these different gendered movements are natural and 'normal'.

Feminist post-structuralist movement pedagogies rely on teachers taking a proactive rather than reactive stance towards children's gendered talk and bodily actions (Blaise, 2009). For instance, instead of reacting to a boy's thundering body movements as he jumps off the bench (see Photograph 6.2) by telling

Photograph 6.2 Multiple bodies. Author's photograph

him either to immediately stop or to move his forceful body somewhere else, a teacher might proactively intervene and find out why he is taking up so much space and how these big and forceful body movements make him feel. In other words, there is an attempt to disclose how power relations, between masculine boy body movements, are working against and marginalizing feminine girl body movements, positioning femininity and masculinity as different and unequal. Another feminist post-structural movement pedagogy that could be used might include a teacher encouraging girls and boys to challenge taken-for-granted stereotypical gender body movements. For instance, a teacher might set up activities that demand girl bodies to be loud, feisty and big in spaces that are often considered 'quiet'. Again, these feminist post-structural movement pedagogies are shifting away from focusing on development and what we assume a body innocently does (i.e. runs, jumps, sits) towards proactively challenging the political gender binaries of quiet/loud, soft/hard, small/big, feminine/masculine that are repeatedly reinforced through the kinds of body movements expected of both girls and boys. Talking with children about gendered body movements is of importance, and finding ways to encourage and support children who want to challenge what a 'girl' or 'boy' body can do is a noteworthy pedagogical move.

Feminist materialist movement pedagogies

Feminist materialism, sometimes referred to as feminist 'new' materialism, insists on the agency and significance of matter (Alaimo, 2016), and it sets out to bring the materiality of the human body (the so-called 'natural' world) and the discursive formation of bodies together, rather than separating them apart. What makes feminist materialism radically different from feminist post-structuralism is the view that the gendered human body does not exist prior to discourse. Rather, gender realities and meanings constantly emerge through discourse *and* materiality, mainly because the human body is always intermeshed with the more-than-human world (Alaimo, 2008). Thus, all sorts of bodies (human and more-than-human) are interconnected, mixed up and entangled.

Developmental and feminist post-structural movement pedagogies both tend to separate the human child body out of the world. For instance, developmentalism sorts out the human child body from the environment by focusing on, categorizing and providing charts and tables of universal child bodies that develop through a set trajectory within an environment. The world is inert and a container of bodies that move through it. When girls sing and move their bodies in provocative and highly sexualized ways to pop songs in their play, developmentalism would be concerned about how these young girls are (appropriately or inappropriately) developing their sense of self as they move to imitate what takes place in their immediate environment. In turn, feminist post-structuralist movement pedagogies acknowledge a fluid body that is constantly shaped through social relations of power. The focus is on the importance of the linguistic, discursive and performative processes that produce gendered bodies. Yet the world continues to be a container for these bodies. Feminist post-structural perspectives would take seriously the girls singing and moving their bodies in provocative and highly sexualized ways to pop songs by unpacking how the girls are performing and negotiating sexualized and gendered movement discourses that they have available to them (Blaise, 2009). In contrast, feminist materialist movement pedagogies consider how gendered bodies emerge (rather than precede) in direct relation with the forces, flows, energies and movements of other (human and non-human) bodies. As Elizabeth Grosz notes, a body is a 'surface of intensities before it is stratified, organized, hierarchized' (1993: 174). These pedagogies actively join both the discursive and the material together and reject an ontology whereby 'things', or in this case bodies, precede their relations (Barad, 2007). Then, we might say that moving girl bodies are becoming through the encounters with music, sexualized discourses and so on. Because we never know what might emerge in this encounter, there is always a political potential that gender can be multiplied rather than reified.

Although there are several ways in which early childhood has taken up feminist materialist perspectives (see Lenz Taguchi, 2014 for an overview; Commonworlds.net for several early childhood inquiries that focus on children's relations with place, other species and materials), we are intrigued and inspired how this approach shifts attention from focusing exclusively on human bodies themselves to the interconnections and entangled relations that always already exist between human and more-than-human bodies. We are encouraged by the material turn, theorized in feminist theory, feminist environmental humanities and feminist science studies, that explores innovative relations within the material world (i.e. Alaimo, 2010a; Barad, 2007; Grosz, 2005; Haraway, 2003). From these perspectives, matter (and in this case, human and more-than-human bodies) are not little separate bits of nature that sit passively outside from the world waiting to be discovered, made significant or mastered; rather they are agentic and inextricably part of the dynamics of the natural world we are all already a part of.

Trans-corporeality, as conceptualized by feminist environmental scholar Stacy Alaimo (2008, 2010a, 2016), helps us make this shift from centring our attention on an individual child's body, body parts and body movements towards overlapping and entangled bodies' relations. From this perspective, all kinds of bodies – that is bodies of thought, child bodies, animal bodies, environmental bodies and so on – are part of the mix. The emphasis on interconnections and movements across bodies also entails movements across different sites. Stacy Alaimo puts it well when she writes about the possibilities of such emphasis:

> By emphasizing the movement across bodies, trans-corporeality reveals the interchanges and interconnections between various bodily natures. But by underscoring that *trans* indicates movement across different sites, trans-corporeality also opens up a mobile space that acknowledges the often unpredictable and unwanted actions of human bodies, nonhuman creatures, ecological systems, chemical agents, and other actors. Emphasizing the material interconnections of human corporeality with the more-than-human world – and, at the same time, acknowledging that material agency necessitates more capacious epistemologies – allows us to forge ethical and political positions that can contend with numerous late twentieth and early twenty-first-century realities in which 'human' and 'environment' can by no means be considered as separate. (2010a: 2)

Both developmental and feminist post-structural movement pedagogies tend to have a pretty good idea of where movements might go, and they focus exclusively on human-child movements. On the other hand, trans-corporeality encourages the unknowable, blurry and indistinct relations between the human and more-than-human world. This shift from focusing on the individual to interconnections and relations across bodies decentres the human subject and refuses notions of a binary logic, boundaries and closures. These refusals of dualisms are at the heart of feminist politics. There is an ethics of unknowability at play, and such a pedagogy requires a feminist objectivity that Donna Haraway (1991) called for over twenty-five years ago, which makes room for the unexpected. A logic of unknowability is part of a feminist materialist movement pedagogy because it is situated and therefore starts from a different place than developmental and feminist post-structural movement pedagogies do. Teachers must make pedagogical decisions that can neither never be certain nor claim to ever get it right. This requires a radically different kind of attitude towards knowledge and meaning making. In other words, a feminist materialist movement pedagogy is never certain about what emerges when human and more-than-human bodies come together, including what gendered bodies might emerge.

Activating feminist materialist movement pedagogies

Enacting a feminist materialist movement pedagogy is not an easy task. There is no recipe or steps to follow. However, in order to do this work requires a logic of unknowability, a logic of openness and a logic of uncertainty. This goes against both developmental and feminist post-structural ideas. Therefore, we do not end with a neat and tidy conclusion of what to do next but instead present a short photo essay as an invitation to consider how a feminist materialist movement pedagogy, which 'thinks with' becoming bodies, emergence and unknowability, might be activated in early childhood education.

The following photos are part of a larger movement inquiry that did not set out to determine how children move (developmental) or to unpack discourses (feminist post-structuralist) embedded in children's movements. Instead, a group of ten preschool children with one educator and two researchers engaged in an investigation of what might emerge through entangled human and more-than-human bodies *moving*. For the period of four months, the children choreographed a performance. Their task was to attend to the way in which their bodies might move with other bodies, how a particular place might become otherwise through (and with) moving bodies and how movement might change them.

Educators and researchers documented the inquiry in collaboration with the children. Rather than photographing how children move through space, children wore a camera (an Autographer) as a way of focusing on what emerges through movement. Here we share a small selection of these photos.

Through each photo, we attempt to highlight the inventive political potential of feminist materialist movement pedagogies to destratify (even if it's only momentarily) gender binaries. We invite readers to pay attention to the reorganization of bodies through human and non-human movements. Our intention is not to erase gender but to multiply gender beyond binary divisions, to traverse gender dominant alignments and to create new connections that destabilize recognition (Grosz, 1993). For instance, paying attention to the unfocused, blurry and undefined bodies in Photographs 6.2–6.4 shakes us out of old habits of thought that work to define girl and boy bodies. Although the encounters we highlight in the photographs might be fleeting and appear insignificant, they embody a sort of political that destratifies gender binaries and 'gendered scenarios of visibility' (Alaimo, 2010b: 18).

These moments also offer possibilities for highlighting the entanglements between human and non-human bodies. For instance, Photographs 6.3–6.5 call us to recognize trans-corporeality, challenge the close demarcation of human bodies and emphasize the always already 'imbrication' of human bodies with physical landscapes. Rather than being called to 'scrutinize' the events 'for shades or shapes of social categorization' (Alaimo, 2010b: 20), they invite us to imagine a body that is not necessarily 'contained by a human frame but extends across the earth' (p. 21). As Stacy Alaimo (2010b) argues, events such as these (see Photographs 6.3–6.5) 'momentarily cast off the boundaries of the human, which allows us to imagine corporeality not as a ground of static substance but as a place of possible connections, interconnections, actions, and ethical becomings' (p. 32).

Challenging the 'shades and shapes of social categorization' is certainly hard but necessary work in early childhood education. We offer the generous words of feminist environmental humanities scholar Astrida Neimanis (2017) as a provocation to 'think with' the series of photos that follow:

> The kinds of ontologies that [a feminist materialism] inaugurates – connected, indebted, dispersed, relational – are not only about correcting a phallogocentric understanding of bodies, but also about developing imaginaries that might allow us to relate differently. (p. 11)

Photograph 6.3 Grassing genders. Author's photograph

Photograph 6.4 Ongoing gender interconnections and exchanges. Author's photograph

Photograph 6.5 Combinations that multiply gender. Author's photograph

Photograph 6.6 Unfixing and unsealing gender. Author's photograph

How might these photographs create otherwise political and ethical action in early childhood education? How might they turn normalized gendered categorizations inside out and upside down? How might they become possibilities for challenging the 'perils of visibility' (Alaimo, 2010b: 23)?

7

(In)conclusion(s): What Gets Produced through Layering Feminist Thought?

Jayne Osgood and Kerry H. Robinson

A Poem of Dis/continuities
Beyond gathering
Exceeds representation
Sensing, mining, navigating
Compose! Orchestrate! Weave!
Intuition, re-turning, remembering, sensing
As child, through child, about child, with child
Why does it matter?
Politic, politik, politicks
Regulation, damnation, liberation
Inclusive, exclusive, abusive
Gender matters, childhood matters, feminism matters
How to tell herstories, histories, they-their-hen-stories?
Worldly stories?
Y/our stories?
They all matter.
Situated, subjugated, standpoint, subaltern
Speak
Act
Sense
Differences matter
Differences materialise
Difficult differences matter.
Margin to centre, decentre, centrifugal forces
Forces, flows, affect-intensities
Productive, generative,
Corporeal bodies, without organs, loathed, loved and transformed

Becoming with dress
Becoming with block
Becoming with movement
Worldling practices
Experiments in (k)not-knowing
Habits, practices, expertise
Wayfaring, uncertainty
Unfolding, infolding and re-turning
Processes that generate
Generations that potentiate
Gender
As
Processes
That
Matter.

Jayne Osgood

This book has attempted to undertake important work; it is as much process as product. The aim of the book was to lay bare our engagements with feminist thought and crucially to capture the long, and at times arduous, processes involved in collaboratively producing knowledge. It has demanded that we revisit, reappraise and re-engage with generations of feminist epistemologies, philosophies and activisms. The book has produced surprises and has unfolded in unanticipated ways through a series of transversal moves and conceptual innovations that challenge conventional conceptions for how we understand and research gender in early childhood. The materialized figuration of this book project has involved deep immersion in waves of feminist thought; through crafting this volume, we have found multiple ways in which to navigate a path through interwoven and multilayered feminist (re)productions of knowledge; there are of course infinite other ways. Through our journey, we have at times stumbled, faltered and stopped dead in our tracks; we have encountered trepidation and dislocation from expert ways of being, sensing and accounting for ourselves and the gendered human child in early childhood contexts. It has been an affective experiment – a generative adventure that has pushed us theoretically, onto-epistemologically and practically.

Threading through the entire experiment has been a desire to challenge the idea that there must be some definitive cut with the past, and instead we argue for the importance of traces and entanglements, threads and knots that bind our feminist projects. Our aim has been to offer a re-turning; processes of re-turning insist upon an openness to re-engage and reimmerse ourselves in the multiple projects of knowledge production that feminist scholars offer to the field of childhood studies. Each chapter can be read in isolation or read diffractively through each other. In many senses, the book has been written diffractively and presents an enactment formed from a more expansive research assemblage. We have worked with a range of feminist philosophers and theorists; therefore, underpinning much of the structure are concepts offered by Butler, Haraway and Barad among others, which have assisted us to undertake intuitive, creative and non-representational research experiments. We have been eager to find ways to bring together feminist post-structuralist thought and method to the more non-representational methodologies deployed by feminist new materialists and explore how together these approaches work hard to move beyond privileging subjective, developmental psychological and reflective interpretations of what we think we know (Coleman & Ringrose, 2013; Koro-Ljungberg et al., 2017; St Pierre & Lather, 2016; St Pierre et al., 2016; Taylor & Hughes, 2016).

> It is a constant challenge for us to rise to the occasion, to catch the wave of life's intensities and ride on it, exposing the boundaries or limits as we transgress them. (Braidotti, 2006: 139)

By attending to waves, wave patterns and overlapping waves in feminist thought and practices in early childhood research, this book has employed practices of diffraction in a quest to map the indebtedness and entanglements of feminist thought and practice and how that produces knowledge about gender in early childhood. We have been concerned to ask 'what else' gets produced through collaborative projects such as this. Working collectively to grapple with how (subjugated, queer) knowledge finds expression in debates about childhood has been messy and, at times, unsettling. Each of us has been pushed in directions that challenge (our) established ways of thinking, sensing and presenting (our) ideas, or as Alaimo (2010c: 20) astutely observes:

> The material self cannot be disentangled from networks that are simultaneously economic, political, cultural, scientific and substantial ... what was once the ostensibly bounded human subject finds herself in a swirling landscape of uncertainties.

The 'swirling landscape of uncertainties' encountered throughout this collaborative project has forced us to engage with the world, and our place as feminist researchers within the world, afresh. Feminist research has long insisted upon the significance of researcher subjectivity and the idea that knowledges are situated (Haraway, 1988). Extending the notion that the researcher is always active in processes of production has opened up possibilities to delve deeper into the significance of matter, time, place, space and context and the ways in which they are interwoven. Decentring the human-child and human-researcher from our investigations into how gender is produced in early childhood has created other ways in which to make sense of what unfolds in the everyday. Haraway has been especially useful to us in reappraising what is possible through our research endeavours. Tracing threads through her corpus of work spanning more than three decades reveals both dis/continuity and complexity. Her insistence that we remain in the thick of things through practices of wayfaring and deep hanging out invites us to reappraise what research might become when we reject any claims to objectivity or impartiality. Her SF philosophy invites a sense of curiosity, wonder and production; by asking the 'what if' questions, we become actively engaged in world-making practices, we are not innocent bystanders gathering representational accounts of the world out there, and rather we are implicated and invested – what we do, how we do it, what we then do with what we have done and what gets produced through the doings demand a heightened sense of response-ability (as has been stressed by feminist philosophers Haraway, Barad and Braidotti).

Revisiting and extending the work that feminist post-structuralism does has revealed the generative potential of addressing the world as material-discursive and recognizing that extending projects of deconstruction and critique can be productive. The questions guiding this project have been: what is especially 'new' about feminist new materialism, and what is especially 'feminist' about feminist new materialism? Throughout this volume. we have wrestled with these concerns, and while we do not reach a neat set of conclusions, it is through practices of foraging, reassembling and composting (Haraway, 2016) – turning over and over, aerating and dislodging – that we have experienced other ways to produce knowledge about gender in early childhood. We have been attuned to the liveliness of matter (Bennett, 2010), and through our investigations, we have sought to explore what gets produced through material-discursive forces, energies, intensities, affects and processes. We have been urged to consider how matter comes to matter which has necessitated working with both familiar and unfamiliar frames.

This book has underlined the importance of blurring boundaries and the possibilities that are presented when we open ourselves to engage with what we thought we knew differently. Attending to everyday habits and practices from queer perspectives has allowed for innovation and creativity.

Kathleen Stewart (2007), in her book *Ordinary Affects*, stresses the productive potential of the everyday, ordinary, habitual, routine and otherwise unremarkable. Early childhood contexts are extraordinarily ordinary, and excessive, and affectively charged. Through this book, we have attended to close examinations of what these extra-ordinary moments, objects, materializations and entanglements make possible when we consider what gender is, where it resides and how it becomes transformed through intra- and inter-actions. Taking 'the dress' and 'dressing up' as one such extra/ordinary materialized practice in early childhood contexts unearthed familiar patterns of knowing, as well as troubling knowledges, but the layering of theoretical lenses produced generative possibilities to deepen our engagements with gender and recognize it as produced and productive, as malleable and as fleeting. Via a careful cartographic exercise of multisensory mapping, it became evident just how deeply and significantly 'the dress' and 'dressing up' come to matter in early childhood contexts. From feminist post-structuralist perspectives, dress-up is constructed as a powerful means through which gendered subjects are rendered intelligible and, furthermore, appreciated for the possibilities it offers children to perform resistance and transgression from binarized, normative gender. Layering a post-humanist analysis enhances the post-structuralist account of why dress-up matters. Working through the affordances of marrying feminist post-structuralism with post-humanism challenges claims for the 'newness' of new materialism. Rather, interweaving a concern with the discursive, material, corporeal and affective in our research investigations produces new knowledge about gender in early childhood because it poses a potentially richer, diffractive set of questions. The dress and dressing up matter, and the coming together of feminist post-structuralism and feminist new materialism is an exercise in attending to the material-discursive, or as Stewart stresses (2007: 1), such investigations might be regarded as experiment rather than judgement

> committed not to the demystification and uncovered truths that support a well-known picture of the world, but rather to speculation, curiosity, and the concrete, it tries to provoke attention to the forces that come into view as habit or shock, resonance or impact. *Something* throws itself together in a moment as an event and a sensation; a something both animated and uninhabitable.

This speculation, curiosity and openness to being attuned to how matter generates forces and affective charges thread throughout the entire book. From revisiting women-only peace camps, we came to revisit the significance of temporality, spatiality and corporeality. Reappraising these spacetimematterings, we identify the ways in which affect and materiality (in both the Marxist and new materialist sense) took, and continue to take, a central role in feminist activism. A concern with affect, bodies and materiality wends and weaves its way through each chapter and exposes what else can be mobilized through feminist investigations of gender when these elements are taken seriously. Each chapter invokes a stutter and a re-turning, re-encountering, remembering and reconfiguring. In the spirit of tracing dis/continuities, I (Jayne) felt an urge to revisit work I had written that was more firmly shaped by feminist post-structuralism. I re-turned to the concluding chapter of *Narratives from the Nursery: Negotiating Professional Identities in Early Childhood* (Osgood, 2012). I recall that the overriding concern then was to identify discourses that I suspected fixed the early years' workforce (as gendered, classed subjects) and so produced particularly narrow subjectivities and discursive positionings. I wondered how I might approach the same study today, whether and how it might be possible to work more attentively with the material and the affective and a sense of not-knowing, investing more deeply in exercises of speculative curiosity. By revisiting the research I undertook over a decade ago, I am struck by the dis/continuities, the political convictions that stand firm, the willingness to trouble and unsettle, and an eagerness to find ways to tell alternative stories about gender in early childhood. The book reaches conclusions with the aid of two quotes concerning minor politics as a collective process of critical thinking; the first is from Rose (1999: 20):

> A matter of introducing a critical attitude towards those things that are given to our present experience as if it were timeless, natural, unquestionable: to stand against the maxim's of one's time, against the spirit of one's age, against the current of received wisdom. It is a matter of introducing awkwardness into the fabric of one's experience, of interrupting the fluency of the narratives that encode that experience, in making them stutter.

The next from Dahlberg and Moss (2005: 151):

> Minor politics involves a *constant critique* and takes a reflective attitude. It is questioning and induces stuttering, disrupting discourses and destabilising accepted meanings, denaturalising the taken for granted, opening up issues to confrontation and contestation. It makes us aware that our constructions are constructions, which are produced in particular contexts and shaped by particular discourses.

The questions shaping my research a decade ago were very firmly shaped by feminist post-structuralism and a concern to critique, problematize and unsettle taken-for-granted truths in order to identify counter discourses through which nursery workers might fabricate alternative ideas about professionalism and ways in which their lives might become more liveable. But it was also a study concerned with biographies, storytelling, interconnections and social (in)justices. These concerns continue to provide justification for undertaking research in early childhood contexts. A feminist new materialist sensibility does not exclude these matters of concern; rather, as the chapters in this book attest, the project becomes more worldly and confederate but no less political. We are invited to rethink thought (Holmes et al., 2018) about both childhood and gender and to consider the other possibilities that are available, that might challenge habitual ways of undertaking research, and to seriously question what counts as data in our investigations. As stressed by Barad (2007) in her agential-realist ontology, the smallest cuts matter; our entangled place within the world presents us with endless opportunities to contend and contest, to interrupt the fluency of dominant modes of thinking and doing, to induce and then stay with the stutter, and to allow space for the stutter to be productive. It is through the minutiae of lives lived in early childhood contexts that we are offered ways to theorize the world, to make a difference and to recognize our small but significant (entangled) place and how a deep immersion in the habitual, ordinary, everyday can produce knowledge and practices that stretch ideas about childhood and gender. As Stewart observes (2007: 2):

> The ordinary is a shifting assemblage of practices and practical knowledges, a scene of both liveliness and exhaustion .... Ordinary affects are the varied, surging capacities to affect and be affected that give everyday life the quality of continual motion of relations, scenes, contingencies and emergencies. They're things that happen.

In a similar vein I, Kerry, encountered demands from this project to grapple with unpublished data (see Chapter 4) as well as revisit my earlier research on queering gender in early childhood and my collaborative research on diversity and difference in early childhood education (Robinson & Criss Jones Diaz, 2006). Despite having written much of this work more than a decade ago, many of the issues associated with gender (and its intersections), discourse and power addressed in these earlier works continue to be as pertinent today as they were then – in some cases, even more so. Feminist post-structuralism provided, and continues to provide, a critical lens through which to identify the tensions, contradictions and relations of power that operate in everyday lives, including those of children. The importance of the discursive-material relationship is especially acute in my work with LGBTQI+ young people and transgender and gender diverse children:

It's like a bird being let out of a cage!

(Transgirl, aged 11, Robinson, Davies, Skinner & Ussher unpublished data)

This research demonstrates that these children and young people, in particular, are pushing the boundaries of normative (hetero)gender, de/stabilising and interrupting what we think we know about gender and its embodiment and materialized configurations. Contradictions abound. Diffractively reading gender through their narratives – demanding different ways of knowing and being – leaves one certain at times, confused at others and always affected.

> The caged bird sings
> with a fearful trill
> of things unknown
> but longed for still
> and his tune is heard
> on the distant hill
> for the caged bird
> sings of freedom.
>
> (Angelou, 1969)

Relationality and the ongoingness of the affective subject

Throughout the processes of crafting this book, we have been variously reminded, through the work of feminist post-structuralists, queer theorists, post-humanists, and indigenous and Aboriginal scholars, of the centrality of relational ways of being, knowing, sensing and becoming and its importance for reaching understandings with and about children and childhood. By way of reaching some sort of a conclusion, we re-turn to Kathleen Stewart's more recent work (2017: 194) and, specifically, her concern with the affective subject. Her invitation to embrace the not-yet-known, and to notice ricocheting and rebounding matters of concern, captures much of what we have attempted in this book, and furthermore, it opens up yet more possible lines of enquiry with which to attend to our ongoing investigations into the mattering of gender in early childhood:

> The subject emerges in the risky labors of being in a world through the precise forms that forces take in lives … The affective subject is a person who waits in the company of others for things to arrive, one who learns to sense out what's

coming and what forms it might take, one who aims to notice what crystallizes and how things ricochet and rebound in a social-natural-aesthetic ecology of compositions and thresholds of expressivity. For the affective subject, there is always the weight of the world in what can be hoped for and what must be feared, in what flourishes and what matters.

References

Åberg, A. & Lenz Taguchi, H. (2005/2018). *Lyssnandets pedagogik. Demokrati och etik i förskolans arbete* [Pedagogy of Listening. Democracy and Ethics in Early Childhood Education]. Stockholm: Liber (translated into Norwegian and Danish).

Ahmed, S. (2006). *Queer Phenomenology: Orientations, Objects, Others*. London: Duke University Press.

Ahmed, S. (2008). Open forum imaginary prohibitions: Some preliminary remarks on the founding gestures of the 'New Materialism'. *European Journal of Women's Studies*, 15 (1): 23–39.

Ahmed, S. (2017). *Living a Feminist Life*. London: Duke University Press.

Alaimo, S. (2008). Trans-corporeal feminisms and the ethical space of nature. In S. Alaimo & S. Hekman (Eds.), *Material Feminisms* (pp. 214–236). Bloomington & Indianapolis: Indiana University Press.

Alaimo, S. (2010a). *Bodily Natures: Science, Environment, and the Material Self*. Bloomington & Indianapolis: Indiana University Press.

Alaimo, S. (2010b). The naked word: The trans-corporeal ethics of the protesting body. *Women & Performance: A Journal of Feminist Theory*, 20 (1): 15–36.

Alaimo, S. (2010c). *Bodily Natures: Science, Environment and the Material Self*. Bloomington: Indiana University Press.

Alaimo, S. (2016). *Exposed: Environmental Politics and Pleasures in Posthuman Times*. Minneapolis: University of Minnesota Press.

Alaimo, S. & Hekman, S. (Eds.) (2008). *Material Feminisms*. Bloomington: Indiana University Press.

Allen, L. & Ingram, T. (2015). 'Bieber Fever': Girls, desire and the negotiation of childhood sexualities. In E. Renold, J. Ringrose, & D. R. Egan(Eds.), *Children, Sexuality and Sexualisation* (pp. 141–158). London: Palgrave Macmillan.

Anastasiou, T. (2018). *Textures of food: Diffracting eating relationships in an early years setting* unpublished PhD thesis. Manchester Metropolitan University.

Angelou, M. (1969). *I Know Why the Cage Bird Sings*. London: Virago Press.

Arnot, M. & Barton, L. (Eds.) (1992). *Voicing Concerns: Sociological Perspectives in Contemporary Education Reforms*. Oxford: Triangle Books. https://files.eric.ed.gov/fulltext/ED365561.pdf#page=58.

Arnot, M. & Weiner, G. (1987) (Eds.) *Gender and the Politics of Schooling*. London: OU press.

Aronsson, L. (submitted). Difference in a different way: A proposal to think otherwise about the desired connection between education and neuroscience.

Aronsson, L. & Lenz Taguchi, H. (2018). Mapping a collaborative cartography of the encounters between the neurosciences and early childhood education practices. *Discourse: Studies in the Cultural Politics of Education*, 39 (2): 242–257.

Askew, S. & Ross, C. (1988). *Boys Don't Cry: Boys and Sexism in Education*. Milton Keynes: Open University Press.

Barad, K. (2003). Posthumanist performativity: Toward an understanding of how matter comes to matter. *Signs*, 28 (3): 801–831.

Barad, K. (2007). *Meeting the Universe Halfway: Quantum Physics and the Entanglement of Matter and Meaning*. Durham and London: Duke University Press.

Barad, K. (2008). Posthumanist performativity: Towards understanding of how matter comes to matter. In Stacy Alaimo & Susan Hekman (Eds.), *Material Feminisms*. Bloomington & Indianapolis: Indiana University Press.

Barad, K. (2010). Quantum entanglements and hauntological relations of inheritance: Dis/continuities, spacetime enfoldings, and justice-to-come. *Derrida Today*, 3 (2): 240–268.

Barad, K. (2012). in Juelskjaer, M. & Schwenessen, N. Intra-active entanglements: An interview with Karen Barad. *Kvinder, Kon og Forskning*, 1 (2): 10–24. http://webcache.googleusercontent.com/search?q=cache:jv7pMin7QAQJ:koensforskning.soc.ku.dk/kkf/forsidebokse/nyeste/interview_karen_barad.pdf+&cd=2&hl=en&ct=clnk&gl=uk&client=safari.

Barry, K. (2016). Transversal travels: The relational movements and environmental intensities of packing a bag. *Studies in Material Thinking: Transversal Practices: Matter, Ecology and Relationality*, 16 (6): 1–16.

Bartlet, A. (2013). Feminist protest in the desert: Researching the 1983 Pine Gap women's peace camp. *Gender, Place & Culture: A Journal of Feminist Geography*, 20 (7): 914–926.

Bates, T. (2015). We have never been Homo sapiens: CandidaHomo naturecultures. *Platform: Journal of Media and Communication*, 6 (2): 16–32.

Bell, D. & Binnie, J. (2000). *The Sexual Citizen: Queer Politics and Beyond*. Cambridge: Polity Press.

Bennett, J. (2001). *The Enchantment of Modern Life. Attachments, Crossings, and Ethics*. Princeton, NJ: Princeton University Press.

Bennett, J. (2010). *Vibrant Matter: A Political Ecology of Things*. USA: Duke University Press.

Berlant, L. (1997). *The Queen of America Goes to Washington City: Essays on Sex and Citizenship*. Durham: Duke University Press.

Berlant, L. (2004). Live sex acts (Parental advisory: Explicit material). In S. Bruhm and N. Hurley (Eds.), *Curiouser: On the Queerness of Children*. Minneapolis: University of Minneapolis Press.

Bhana, D. (2008).Discourses of childhood innocence in primary school HIV/AIDS education in South Africa. *African Journal of AIDS Research*, 7 (1): 149–158.

Blair, S. & Rillo M. (2016). *Serious Work: How to Facilitate Lego Serious Play Meetings and Workshops*. ProMeet, London (ISBN 978-0995664708).

Blaise, M. (2005a). *Playing It Straight: Uncovering Gender Discourse in the Early Childhood Classroom*. New York: Routledge.

Blaise, M. (2005b). A feminist poststructuralist study of children 'doing' gender in an urban kindergarten classroom. *Early Childhood Research Quarterly*, 20 (1): 85–108.

Blaise, M. (2009). 'What a girl wants, what a girl needs!': Responding to sex, gender, and sexuality in the early childhood classroom. *Journal of Research in Childhood Education*, 23 (4): 450–460.

Blaise, M. (2010). Kiss and tell: Gendered narratives and childhood sexuality. *Australasian Journal of Early Childhood*, 35 (1): 1–9.

Blaise, M. (2013a). Activating micro-political practices in the early years: (Re) assembling *bodies and participant observations*. In R. Coleman & J. Ringrose (Eds.), *Deleuze and Research Methodologies* (pp. 184–201). Edinburgh: Edinburgh University Press.

Blaise, M. (2013b). Gender discourses and play. In L. Brooker, M. Blaise, & S. Edwards (Eds.), *The SAGE Handbook of Play and Learning in Early Childhood* (pp. 115–127). London: SAGE.

Braidotti, R. (2006). The ethics of becoming imperceptible. In C. V. Boundas (Ed.), *Deleuze & Philosophy*. Edinburgh: Edinburgh University Press.

Braidotti, R. (2013). *The Posthuman*. Cambridge: Polity Press.

British Broadcasting Corporation (2017). *No More Boys & Girls: Can Our Kids Go Gender Free?* http://www.bbc.co.uk/programmes/b09202lp broadcast 12th September 2017.

Browne, N. & France, P. (1986). *Untying the Apron Strings: Anti-sexist Provision for the Under Fives*. Milton Keynes: Open University Press.

Bruhm, S. & Hurley, N. (2004).'Curiouser: On the queerness of children'. In S. Bruhm & N. Hurley(Eds.), *Curiouser: On the Queerness of Children*. Minneapolis: University of Minneapolis Press.

Bürgi, P. & Roos, J. (2003). Images of strategy. *European Management Journal*, 21 (1): 69–78.

Bürgi, P., Jacobs, C., & Roos, J. (2005). From metaphor to practice in the crafting of strategy. *Journal of Management Inquiry*, 14 (1): 78–94.

Burman, E. (1994). *Deconstructing Developmental Psychology*. London: Routledge.

Burman, E. (2008). *Developments: Child, Image, Nation*. London: Routledge.

Burt, T., Gelnaw, A., & Lesser, L. K. (2010). Creating welcoming and inclusive environments for lesbian, gay, bisexual and transgender (LGBT) families in early childhood settings. http://www.naeyc.org/files/yc/file/201001/LesserWeb0110.pdf.

Butler, J. (1990). *Gender Trouble: Feminism and the Subversion of Identity*. New York: Routledge.

Butler, J. (1993). *Bodies that Matter: On the Discursive Limits of 'Sex'*. New York: Routledge.

Butler, J. (1994). Gender as performance: An interview with Judith Butler. *Radical Philosophy*, 67: 32–39.

Butler, J. (2004a). *Undoing Gender*. New York: Routledge.

Butler, J. (2004b). *Precarious Life. The Powers of Mourning and Violence*. New York: Verso.

Cannella, G. S. (1997). *Deconstructing Early Childhood Education: Social Justice and Revolution*. New York: Peter Lang.

Cannella, G. S. & Viruru, R. (2004). *Childhood and Postcolonialization*. New York: Routledge Falmer.

Colebrook, C. (2000). Introduction. In Ian Buchanan & Claire Colebrook (Ed.), *Deleuze and Feminist Theory*. Edinburgh: Edinburgh University Press.

Colebrook, C. (2012). *Extinction*. Open Humanities Press. http://www.livingbooksaboutlife.org/books/Extinction

Colebrook, C. (2013). Is the Anthropocene … a doomsday device? http://www.hkw.de/en/programm/2013/anthropozaen/multimedia_anthropozaen/video_anthropozaen/video_anthropozaen.php

Colebrook, C. (2014). *Sex after Life: Essays on Extinction, Vol. 2*. Open Humanities Press.

Coole, D. & Frost, S. (2010). *New Materialism: Ontology, Agency & Politics*. Durham, NC: Duke University Press.

Corteen, K. & Scraton, P. (1997). 'Prolonging "childhood", manufacturing "innocence" and regulating sexuality'. In P. Scraton (Ed.), *'Childhood' in 'Crisis'*. London: University College London Press.

Crain, W. (2011). *Theories of Development: Concepts and Applications*, 6th Edition. Boston, MA: Prentice Hall.

Crenshaw, K. (1989). Demarginalizing the intersection of race and sex: A black feminist critique of antidiscrimination doctrine, feminist theory and antiracist politics. *University of Chicago Legal Forum*, 1989, Article 8.

Cresswell, T. (1994). Putting women in their place: The carnival at Greenham Common. *Antipode*, 26 (1): 35–58.

Dahlberg, G. & Moss, P. (2005). *Thics and Politics in Early Childhood Education*. London: Routledge.

The Daily Telegraph (2017). Lego sales crumble as children turn away from building bricks. https://www.telegraph.co.uk/business/2017/09/05/lego-sales-crumble-children-turn-away-building-bricks/ (accessed 23 December 2017).

David, M. (1992). Parents & the State. In M. Arnot & L. Barton (Eds.), *Voicing Concerns: Sociological Perspectives in Contemporary Education Reforms* (pp. 1–19). Oxford: Triangle Books.

Davies, B. (1989). *Frogs and Snails and Feminist Tales: Preschool Children and Gender*. Sydney: Allen & Unwin.

Davies, B. (1993). *Shards of Glass: Children Reading and Writing beyond Gendered Identities*. Sydney: Allen & Unwin.

Davies, B. (2010). The implications for qualitative research methodology of the struggle between the individualised subject of phenomenology and the emergent multiplicities of the poststructuralist subject: The problem of agency. *Reconceptualizing Educational Research Methodology*, 1 (1). http://www.rerm.hio. no.

Davies, B. (2014). *Listening to Children: Being and Becoming*. London: Routledge.

Davies, B. (2018). Ethics and the new materialism: A brief genealogy of the 'post' philosophies in the social sciences. *Discourse: Studies in the Cultural Politics of Education*, 39 (1): 113–127.

Davies, C. (2008). Becoming sissy. In B. Davies (Ed.), *Judith Butler in Conversation: Analysing the Texts and Talk of Everyday Life* (pp. 117–133). New York: Routledge.

Davies, C. & Robinson, K. H. (2010). Hatching babies and stork deliveries: Risk and regulation in the construction of children's sexual knowledge. *Contemporary Issues in Early Childhood*, 11 (3): 249–262.

Davies, C. & Robinson, K.H. (2012). *Reflective Practice with Early and Middle Childhood Education and Care Professionals*. Child Australia, WA.

Davis, B. (1997). The subject of post-structuralism: A reply to Alison Jones. *Gender and Education*,9(3): 271–283.

Davis, T. (2016). 'Before European Christians Forced Gender Roles, Native Americans Acknowledged 5 Genders' (accessed 8 April 2018). http://bipartisanreport. com/2016/06/19/before-european-christians-forced-gender-roles-native-americans-acknowledged-5-genders/.

De Beauvoir, S. (1949). *The Second Sex*. London: Vintage Books.

De Lauretis, T. (1987). *Technologies of Gender: Essays on Theory, Film and Fiction*. Indiana University Press. Dispatchwork (2016). https://www.janvormann.com/ testbild/dispatchwork/

Deleuze, G. & Guattari, F. (1987). *A Thousand Plateaus. Capitalism and Schizophrenia*. Minneapolis: University of Minnesota Press.

Diamond, M. C., Krech, D., & Rosenzweig, M. R. (1964). The effects of an enriched environment on the histology of the rat cerebral cortex. *Journal of Comparative Neurology*, 123 (1): 111–119.

Drew, W., Christie, J., Johnson, J., Meckley, A., & Nell. M. (2008). Constructive Play. *NAEYC Young Child*, 38–44, July.

Egan, D. R. & Hawkes, G. (2010). *Theorizing the Sexual Child in Modernity*. New York: Palgrave Macmillan.

Eidevald, C. & Lenz Taguchi, H. (2011). Genuspedagogik och förskolan som jämställdhetspolitisk arena. In Lenz Taguchi, Bodén and Ohrlander (Eds.), *En rosa pedagogik. Jämställdhetspedagogiska Utmaningar*. Stockholm: Liber.

Elkin Postila, T. (submitted). Water as method: Explorations of locally situated environmental issues together with pre-schoolers.

Epstein, D. (1995). 'Girls don't do bricks': Gender and sexuality in the primary classroom. In J.& I. Siraj-Blatchford (Eds.), *Educating the Whole Child: Cross-curricula Skills, Themes and Dimensions* (pp. 56–69). Buckingham: Open University Press.

Faludi, S. (1994). *Backlash. The Undeclared War against Women*. Vintage.

Fausto-Sterling, A. (2000). *Sexing the Body: Gender Politics and the Construction of Sexuality*. New York: Basic Books.

Fforde, C., Bamblett, L., Lovett, R., Gorringe, S., & Fogarty, W. (2013). Discourse, deficit and identity: Aboriginality, the race paradigm and the language of representation in contemporary Australia. *Media International Australia*, 149: 162–173.

Fields, Jessica. (2008). *Risky Lessons: Sex Education and Social Inequality*. New Brunswick, NJ: Rutgers University Press.

Fields, J. & Payne, E. (2016). Editorial introduction: Gender and sexuality taking up space in schooling. *Sex Education*, 16 (1): 1–7.

Fine, C. & Rush, E. (2016). 'Why do all the girls have to buy pink stuff?' The ethics and science of the gendered toy marketing debate. *Journal of Business Ethics*, 149 (4): 1–16.

Flax, J. (1993). *Disputed Subjects. Essays on Psychoanalysis, Politics and Philosophy*. New York and London: Routledge.

Foucault, M. (1974). *The Archaeology of Knowledge*. London: Tavistock.

Foucault, M. (1980). *Power/Knowledge: Selected Interviews and Other Writings 1972–1977*. New York: Pantheon Books.

Fox, N. J. & Alldred, P. (2017). New materialism. In P. A. Atkinson S. Delamont, M. A. Hardy, & M. Williams (Eds.), *The Sage Encyclopedia of Research Methods*. London: Sage.

Fox Keller, E. (1989). The gender/science system: Or, is sex to gender as nature is to science. In Nancy Tuana (Ed.), *Feminism and Science*. Bloomington: Indiana University Press.

Francis, B. (1998). *Power Plays: Primary School Children's Constructions of Gender, Power and Adult Work*. London: Trentham Books.

Frankenberg, S., Lenz Taguchi, H., Gerholm, T., Bodén, L., Kallioinen, P., Kjällander, S., Palmer, A., & Tonér, S. (2018). Bidirectional collaborations in an intervention RCT study performed in the Swedish early childhood education context. *Journal of Cognition and Development* (to be published online shortly).

Fraser, N. (1992). Rethinking the public sphere: A contribution to the critique of actually existing democracy. In C. Calhoun (ed.), *Habermas and the Public Sphere*. Cambridge, MA: MIT press.

Gailor (2016). Lego lost at sea. *Ernest Journal: Curiosity & Adventure*, (4): 34–38, May.

Gallahue, D. L., Ozmun, J. C., Goodway, J. D. (2012). *Understanding Motor Development: Infants, Children, Adolescents, Adults*, 7th Edition. New York: McGraw-Hill.

Gannon, S. (2017). Saving Squawk? Animal and human entanglement at the edge of the lagoon. *Environmental Education Research*, 23 (1): 91–110.

García, A. M. & Slesaransky-Poe (2010). The heteronomative classroom: Questioning and liberating practices. *The Teacher Educator*, 45 (4): 244–256.

Geist, E. (2009). Infants and toddlers exploring mathematics. *NAEYC Young Child*, 39–41, May.

Gewirtz, S., Ball, S. J., & Bowe, R. (1995). *Markets, Choice and Equity in Education*. Buckingham: Open University Press.

Gilbert, J. (2014). *Sexuality in School: The Limits of Education*. Minneapolis: University of Minnesota Press.

Gittins, D. (1998). *The Child in Question*. London: Macmillan.

Goldman, R. & Goldman, J. (1982). *Children's Sexual Thinking. A Comparative Study of Children Aged 5 to 15 Years in Australia, North America, Britain and Sweden*. London: Routledge & Kegan Paul.

Greishaber, S. (1998). Constructing the gendered infant. In N. Yelland (Ed.), *Gender in Early Childhood* (pp. 15–35). London: Routledge.

Greytak, E. A., Kosciw, J. G., & Diaz, E. M. (2009). *Harsh Realities*. New York: GLSEN.

Grosz, E. (1993). A thousand tiny sexes: Feminism and rhizomatics. *Topoi*, 12: 167–179.

Grosz, E. (1994). *Volatile Bodies: Toward a Corporeal Feminism*. Bloomington and Sydney: Indiana University Press and Allen & Unwin.

Grosz, E. (2005). *Time Travels: Feminism, Nature, Power*. Australia: AllenUnwin.

The Guardian (2013). https://www.theguardian.com/uk-news/2013/sep/02/greenham-common-women-taught-generation-protest (accessed 15 December 2016).

Halberstam, J. (1998). *Female Masculinity*. Durham, NC: Duke University Press.

Hall, S. (1988). *The Hard Road to Renewal: Thatcherism and the Crisis of the Left*. London: Verso.

Haraway, D. (1991). *Simians, Cyborgs, and Women*. New York and London: Routledge and Free Association Books.

Haraway, D. (1992). The promises of monsters: A regenerative politics inappropriated others. In Lawrence Grossberg, Cory Nelson, & Paula Treichler (Eds.), *Cultural Studies* (pp. 295–337). New York: Routledge.

Haraway, D. (2016). *Staying with the Trouble: Making Kin in the Chthulucene*. London: Duke University Press.

Haraway, D. J. (1988). Situated knowledges: The science question in feminism and the privilege of partial perspective. *Feminist Studies*, 14 (3) (Autumn 1988): 575–599.

Haraway, D. J. (1989). *Primate Visions: Gender, Race, and Nature in the World of Modern Science*. London: Routledge.

Haraway, D. J. (1994). A game of cat's cradle: Science studies, feminist theory, cultural studies. *Configurations*, 2 (1): 59–71.

Haraway, D. J. (2003). *The Haraway Reader*. London: Routledge.

Haraway, D. J. (2008). *When Species Meet*. Minneapolis: University of Minnesota Press.

Haraway, D. J. (2015). Anthropocene, Capitalocene, Plantationocene, Chthulucene: Making Kin. *Environmental Humanities*, 6 (1): 159–165. doi: https://doi.org/10.1215/22011919-3615934.

Harms, T., Cryer, D., & Riley, C. (2003a). *All about the ITERS-R*. New York: Kaplan Learning Company.

Harms, T., Cryer, D., & Riley, C. (2003b). *All about the ECERS- R*. New York: Kaplan Early Learning Company.

Hekman, S. (1990). *Gender and Knowledge. Elements of Postmodern Feminism.* Cambridge and Oxford: Polity Press.

Hekman, S. (2010). *The Material of Knowledge: Feminist Disclosures.* Bloomington: Indiana University Press.

Herbert, J. (2005). 'Owning the Discourse: Seizing the Power!'. Paper presented at AARE 2005 Conference, 'Education Research: Creative Dissent: Constructive Solutions', The University of Western Sydney, Parramatta Campus, Sydney, NSW, Australia 27–30 November (accessed April 2018). https://www.aare.edu.au/data/publications/2005/her05217.pdf.

Hickey-Moody, A. C. (2017). Arts practice as method, urban spaces and intra-active faiths'. *International Journal of Inclusive Education.* 1–14. doi:10.1080/13603116.2017.1350317.

Holford, N., Renold, E., & Huuki, T. (2013). What (else) can a kiss do? Theorizing the power plays in young children's sexual cultures. *Sexualities,* 16 (5–6): 710–729.

Holmes, R., Jones, L., & Osgood, J. (in press, 2018). Mundane habits and methodological creations. In A. Cutter-Mackenzie, K. Malone, and E. Barratt Hacking (Eds.), *International Research Handbook on ChildhoodNature.* Switzerland: Spring Nature.

Honig, A. (1983). Sex role socialisation in early childhood. *Young Children,* 38 (6): 57–70.

hooks, b. (1981). *Ain't I a Woman?: Black Women and Feminism.* Boston, MA: South End Press.

hooks, b. (1982). *Black Looks: Race and Representation.* Boston, MA: South End Press.

hooks, b. (1984). *Feminist Theory: From Margin to Center.* Boston, MA: South End Press.

Hughes, C. & Lury, C. (2013). Re-turning feminist methodologies: From a social to an ecological epistemology. *Gender & Education Journal,* 25 (6): 786–799. doi: 10.1080/09540253.2013.829910

Hultman, K. & Lenz Taguchi, H. (2010). Challenging anthropocentric analysis of visual data: A relational materialist methodological approach to educational research. *International Journal of Qualitative Studies in Education,* 23 (5): 525–542.

Huuki, T. & Renold, E. (2015). 'Crush: Mapping historical, material and affective force relations in young children's hetero-sexual playground play. *Discourse: Studies in the Cultural Politics of Education.* doi:10.1080/01596306.2015.1075730.

Jackson, S. (1982). *Childhood and Sexuality.* Oxford: Blackwell.

Jarvis, K. & Sandretto, S. (2010). The power of discursive practices: Queering or heteronormalising? *New Zealand Research in Early Childhood Education,* 13: 43–56.

Jayne, C. F. (1906). *String Figures and How to Make Them: A Study of Cat's Cradle in Many Lands.* http://www.stringfigures.info/cfj/real-cats-cradle.html, translation by Jamis Buck (2009).

Jones, A. (1993). Becoming a 'girl': Post-structuralist suggestions for educational research. *Gender and Education,* 5(2): 157–166.

Jones, L. (2013). Becoming child/Becoming dress. *Global Studies of Childhood*, 3 (3): 289–296.

Juelskjaer, M. (2013). Gendered subjectivities of spacetimematter. *Gender and Education*, 25 (6): 754–768.

Juelskjaer, M. & Schwenessen, N. (2012). Intra-active entanglements: An interview with Karen Barad. *Kvinder, Kon og Forskning*, 1 (2): 10–24.

Kennedy, J. (2014). How are Lego® bricks made? The Chemistry of LEGO®. https://jameskennedymonash.wordpress.com/2014/07/15/how-are-lego-bricks-made-the-chemistry-of-lego/.

Kidron, B. (2007). Your Greenham. *The Guardian* (accessed 22 September 2017).

Kilodavis, C. (2009). *My Princess Boy*. USA: KD Talent LLC Principals and Publisher.

Kincaid, J. (2004). Producing erotic children. In S. Bruhm & N. Hurley (Eds.), *Curiouser: On the Queerness of Children*. Minneapolis: University of Minneapolis Press.

Kind, S. (2013). Lively entanglements: The doings, movements and enactments of photography. *Global Studies of Childhood*, 3 (4): 427–441.

Kitzinger, J. (1990). Who are you kidding? Children, power and the struggle against sexual abuse. In A. James & A. Prout (Eds.), *Constructing and Reconstructing Childhood: Contemporary Issues in the Sociological Study of Childhood*. London: The Falmer Press.

Koro-Ljungberg, M., Lotyonen, T., & Tesar, M. (2017). *Disrupting Data in Qualitative Inquiry: Entanglements with the Post-critical and Post-anthropocentric*. London: Peter Lang.

Langton, M. (1998). 'Speaking Their Minds'. Speaking Their Minds. Intellectuals and the Public Culture in Australia. R. Dessaix. Sydney, ABC:231.

Lather, P. (1993). Fertile obsession: Validity after poststructuralism. *The Sociological Quarterly*, 34 (4): 673–693.

Lather, P. & E. A. St. Pierre (2013). Post-qualitative inquiry. *International Journal of Qualitative Studies in Education*, 26 (6): 629–633.

Latour, B. (2004). *Politics of Nature: How to Bring the Sciences into Democracy*. Translated by Catherine Porter. Cambridge, MA: Harvard University Press.

Le Guin, U. (1986). *The Carrier Bag Theory of Fiction*. New York: Grove Press.

The Lego Group (2016). *Responsibility Report*. https://www.lego.com/en-us/aboutus/responsibility/our-policies-and-reporting/responsibility-report-2016-downloads (accessed 13 June 2017).

Lenz Taguchi, H. (1997/2013). *Varför pedagogisk dokumentation?* [Why Pedagogical Documentation?], 2nd Edition. Malmö: Gleerups.

Lenz Taguchi, H. (2000). *Emancipation och motstånd. Dokumentation och kooperativa läroprocesser i förskolan* [Emancipation and resistance. Documentation practices and co-operative learning-processes in early childhood education.] Stockholm. HLS Förlag. Published PhD dissertation.

Lenz Taguchi, H. (2004/2013). *In på bara benet. Introduktion till feministisk poststrukturalism* [Down to bare down. Introduction to feminist post-structuralism], 2nd Edition. Malmö: Gleerups. (Reviderad 2013. Överstatt till norska på Universitetsförlaget 2015).

Lenz Taguchi, H. (2007). Deconstructing and transgressing the theory – Practice dichotomy in Swedish early childhood education. *Educational Philosophy and Theory*, 39 (3): 275–290.

Lenz Taguchi, H. (2008). An 'ethics of resistance' challenges taken-for-granted ideas in early childhood education. *International Journal of Educational Research*, 47 (5): 270–282.

Lenz Taguchi, H. (2010). *Going beyond the Theory/Practice Divide in Early Childhood Education: Introducing an Intra-active Pedagogy*. London and New York: Routledge.

Lenz Taguchi, H. (2012). A diffractive and Deleuzian approach to analysing interview data. *Feminist Theory*, 13 (3): 265–281.

Lenz Taguchi, H. (2013). Images of thinking in feminist materialisms: Ontological divergences and the production of researcher subjectivities. *International Journal of Qualitative Studies in Education*, 26 (6): 706–716.

Lenz Taguchi, H. (2014). New materialisms and play. In L. Brooker, M. Blaise, & S. Edwards (Eds.), *The SAGE Handbook of Play and Learning in Early Childhood* (pp. 79–90). London: SAGE.

Lenz Taguchi, H. (2017). 'This is not a photograph of a fetus': A feminist reconfiguration of the concept of posthumanism as the ultrasound fetus image, i *Qualitative Inquiry*, 23 (9).

Lenz Taguchi, H. & Palmer, A. (2013). A diffractive methodology to 'disclose' possible realities of girls' material-discursive health/'wellbeing' in school-settings. Invited article to *Gender and Education*, 25 (6): 671–687.

Liinason, M. (2011). The construction of gender research in Sweden: An analysis of a success story. SQS: *Journal of Queer Studies in Finland*, 2: 30–43. https://journal.fi/sqs/index.

Lipkowitz, D. (2011). *The Lego Ideas Book: You Can Build Anything*. London: Dorling Kindersley under licence from The Lego Group.

Lippmann, L. (1994). *Generations of Resistance: Mabo and Justice*. Melbourne: Longman Cheshire.

Lloro-Bidart, T. (2017). A feminist posthumanist political ecology of education for theorizing human-animal relations/relationships. *Environmental Education Research*, 23 (1): 111–130.

Lorde, A. (1984). *Sister Outsider: Essays and Speeches*. Freedom, CA: Crossing Press.

Lorimer, H. (2005). Cultural geography: The busyness of being 'more-than-representational'. *Progress in Human Geography*, 29: 83–94.

Lupton, D. (1992). Discourse analysis: A new methodology for understanding the ideologies of health and illness. *Australian Journal of Public Health*, 16 (2): 145–150.

Lykke, N. (2010). *Feminist Studies. A Guide to Intersectional Theory, Methodology and Writing*. New York and Oxon: Routledge.

Lyttleton-Smith, J. (2015). *Becoming gendered bodies: A posthuman analysis of how gender is produced in an early childhood classroom* (unpublished PhD thesis). Cardiff University.

Lyttleton-Smith, J. (2017). Objects of conflict: (re)Configuring early childhood experiences of gender in the preschool classroom [online]. *Gender and Education*, 1–18. doi:10.1080/09540253.2017.1332343.

Maccoby, E. E. and Jacklin, C. (1974). *The Psychology of Sex Differences*. Stanford, CA: Stanford University Press.

MacLure, M. (2013). The wonder of data. *Cultural Studies* ← → *Critical Methodologies*, 13 (4): 228–232.

MacNaughton, G. (2000). *Rethinking Gender in Early Childhood Education*. Sydney: Allen & Unwin.

Macrae, C. (2012). Encounters with a life(less) baby doll: Rethinking relations of agency through a collectively lived moment. *Contemporary Issues in Early Childhood*, 13 (2): 120–131.

Manning, E. (2014). Wondering the world directly – Or how movement outruns the subject. *Body and Society*, 20 (3&4): 162–188.

Manning, E. (2016). *The Minor Gesture*. Durham, North Carolina: Duke University Press.

Martin, K. L. (2008). *Please Knock before You Enter: Aboriginal Regulation of Outsiders and the Implications for Researchers*. Teneriffe, Australia: Post Pressed.

Mazzei, L. A. (2013). Materialist mappings of knowing in being: Researchers constituted in the production of knowledge. *Gender and Education*, 25 (6): 776–785.

McKnight, L. (2015). Still in the LEGO (LEGOS) room: Female teachers designing curriculum around girls' popular culture for the coeducational classroom in Australia. *Gender & Education*, 27 (7): 909–927.

McRobbie, A. (1994). *Postmodernism and Popular Culture*. London: Routledge.

Moberg, E. (2018). Children, sub-headings and verbal discussions creating evaluations: Acknowledging the productiveness of ambivalence. *Pedagogy, Culture & Society*, 26 (3): 363–379. doi: 10.1080/14681366.2017.1403951.

Mohanty, C. T. (1991). Under western eyes: Feminist scholarship and colonial discourses. In C. T. Mohanty, A. Russo, & L. Torres (Eds.), *Third World Women and the Politics of Feminism* (pp. 255–277). Bloomington: Indiana University Press.

Mol, A. (2008). I Eat an Apple. On Theorizing Subjectivities. *Subjectivity*, 22: 28–37.

Money, J. & Ehrhardt, A. A. (1972). *Man and Woman, Boy and Girl: The Differentiation and Dimorphism of Gender Identity from Conception to Maturity*. Baltimore, MD: John Hopkins University Press.

Moreton-Robinson, A. (2009). Imagining the good indigenous citizen: Race war and the pathology of patriarchal white sovereignty. *Cultural Studies Review*, 15 (2): 61–79.

Moreton-Robinson, A. (2017). Senses of Belonging: How Indigenous Sovereignty Unsettles White Australia. ABC Religion and Ethics, 21 February (accessed April 2018). http://www.abc.net.au/religion/articles/2017/02/21/4623659.htmhttp://www.abc.net.au/religion/articles/2017/02/21/4623659.htmhttp://www.abc.net.au/religion/articles/2017/02/21/4623659.htmhttp://www.abc.net.au/religion/articles/2017/02/21/4623659.htm.

Moss, P., Dahlberg, G., & Pence, A. (1999/2013). *Beyond Quality in Early Childhood Education and Care: Languages of Evaluation*. Routledge.

Moxnes, A. & Osgood, J. (2018). Sticky stories from the classroom: From reflection to diffraction in early childhood teacher education. *Contemporary Issues in Early Childhood*. https://doi.org/10.1177/1463949118766662.

Murris, K. (2017). *The Posthuman Child*. London: Routledge.

Neimanis, A. (2017). *Bodies of Water: Posthuman Feminist Phenomenology*. London: Bloomsbury.

Newman, S. D., Hansen, M. T., & Gutierrez, A. (2016). An fMRI study of the impact of block building and board games of spatial ability. *Frontiers in Psychology*, 7: 1278.

Nordlander, J. (2018). *Mellan raderna. En bok om att vara kvinna och journalist.* [Between the Lines. A Book about Being a Woman and a Journalist]. Stockholm: Natur och Kultur.

Nxumalo, F. (2016). Storying practices of witnessing: Refiguring quality in everyday pedagogical encounters. *Contemporary Issues in Early Childhood Journal*, 17 (1): 39–53.

Olsson, L. (2009). *Movement and Experimentation in Young Children's Learning: Deleuze and a Virtual Child*. London and New York: Routledge.

Olsson, L. M. (2013). Taking children's questions seriously: The need for creative thought. *Global Studies of Childhood*, 3 (3): 230–253.

Osgood, J. (2012). *Narratives from the Nursery: Negotiating Professional Identities in Early Childhood*. London: Routledge.

Osgood, J. (2014). Playing with gender: Making space for posthuman childhood(s). In J. Moyles, J. Payler, & J. Georgeson (Eds.), *Early Years Foundations: Critical Issues* (pp. 191–202). Maidenhead: Open University Press.

Osgood, J. (2015a). Reimaging gender and play. In J. Moyles (Ed.), *The Excellence of Play* (pp. 49–60). Maidenhead: Open University Press.

Osgood, J. (2015b). Postmodernist theorising in early childhood education and care: Making the familiar strange in pursuit of social justice. In T. David, K. Goouch, & S. Powell (Eds.), *The Routledge International Handbook of Philosophies and Theories of Early Childhood Education and Care* (pp. 157–164). London: Taylor & Francis.

Osgood, J. (2018, in press). Queering understandings of how matter comes to matter in the baby room. In L. Moran, K. Reilly, & B. Brady (Eds.), *Narrating Childhoods across Contexts: Knowledge, Environment and Relationships*. London: Palgrave MacMillan.

Osgood J. & Robinson, K. H. (2017). Celebrating pioneering and contemporary feminist approaches to studying gender in early childhood. In K. Smith, K. Alexander, & S. Campbell (Eds.), *Feminisms in Early Childhood: Using Feminist Theories in Research and Practice* (pp. 35–47). Singapore, Springer Nature: Springer.

Osgood, J., Scarlet, R. R. & Bhopal, K. (2016). Reconfiguring motherhoods: transmogrifying the maternal entanglements of feminist academics. In K.A. Scott & A.S. Henwood (Eds.), *Women Education Scholars and Their Children's Schooling*. London: Routledge.

Pacini-Ketchabaw, V. (2012). Acting with the clock: Clocking practices in early childhood education. *Contemporary Issues in Early Childhood*, 13 (2): 154–160.

Paechter, C. & Clark, S. (2007). Who are tomboys and how do we recognize them? *Women's Studies International Forum*, 30: 342–354.

Palmer, A. (2011). 'How many sums can I do?' Performative strategies and diffractive thinking as methodological tools for rethinking mathematical subjectivity. *Reconceptualizing Educational Research Methodology*, 1 (1): 3–18.

Pasulka, N. (2015). Ladies in the streets: Before Stonewall, Transgender uprising changed lives. https://www.npr.org/sections/codeswitch/2015/05/05/404459634/ ladies-in-the-streets-before-stonewall-transgender-uprising-changed-lives.

Pink, S., Sumartojo, S., Lupton, D., & Heyes LaBond, C. (2017). Empathetic technologies: Digital materiality and video ethnography. *Visual Studies*, 32 (4): 371–381.

Pitts-Taylor, V. (2016). *The Brain's Body. Neuroscience and Corporeal Politics*. Durham and London: Duke University Press.

Prosser, J. (2013). Judith Butler: Queer feminism, transgender, and the transubstantiation of sex. In D. E Hall, A. Jagose, A. Bebell, & S. Potter (Eds.), *The Routledge Queer Studies Reader* (pp. 32–59). London: Routledge.

Pyyry, N. (2016). Learning with the city via enchantment: Photo-walks as creative encounters. *Discourse: Studies in the Cultural Politics of Education*, 37: 102–115.

Reay, D. (2001). 'Spice Girls', 'Nice Girls', 'Girlies' and 'Tomboys': Gender discourse girls' cultures and femininities in the primary classroom. *Gender and Education*, 13 (2): 153–166.

Renold, E. (2005). *Girls, Boys and Junior Sexualities: Exploring Children's Gender and Sexual Relations in the Primary School*. London: RoutledgeFalmer.

Renold, E. (2006) 'They won't let us play…unless you're going out with them': Girls, boys and Butler's 'heterosexual matrix' in the primary years. *British Journal of Sociology of Education*, 27 (4): 489–509.

Renold, E. & Mellor, D. (2013). Deleuze and Guattari in the nursery: Towards an ethnographic, multi-sensory mapping of gendered bodies and becomings. In R. Coleman & J. Ringrose (Eds.), *Deleuze and Research Methodologies* (pp. 23–41). Edinburgh: Edinburgh University Press.

Richardson, D. (1998). Sexuality and citizenship. *Sociology*, 32 (1): 83–100.

Ringrose, J., Renold, E., & Regan, D. (Eds.) (2015). *Children, Sexuality and Sexualization*. London: Palgrave.

Robinson, K. H. (2005). 'Queerying' gender: Heteronormativity in early childhood education. *Australian Journal of Early Childhood*, 30 (2): 19–28.

Robinson, K. H. (2008). In the name of 'childhood innocence'. A discursive exploration of the moral panic associated with childhood and sexuality. *Cultural Studies Review*, 14 (2): 113–129.

Robinson, K. H. (2012a). Difficult citizenship: The precarious relationships between childhood, sexuality and access to knowledge. *Sexualities*, 15 (3/4): 257–276.

Robinson, K. H. (2012b). Childhood as a 'queer time and space': Alternative imaginings of normative markers of gendered lives. In K. H. Robinson & C. Davies (Eds.), *Queer and Subjugated Knowledges: Generating Subversive Imaginaries*. United Emirates: Bentham eBooks.

Robinson, K. H. (2013). *Innocence, Knowledge and the Construction of Childhood: The Contradictory Nature of Sexuality and Censorship in Children's Contemporary Lives.* London: Routledge.

Robinson, K. H. & Davies, C. (2007). Tomboys and Sissy Girls: Young girls' negotiations of femininity and masculinity. *International Journal of Equity and Innovation in Early Childhood*, 5 (2): 17–31.

Robinson, K. H. & Davies, C. (2008a). She's kickin' ass, that's what she's doing: Deconstructing childhood 'innocence' in media representations. *Australian Feminist Studies*, 23 (57): 343–358.

Robinson, K. H. & Davies, C. (2008b). Docile bodies and heteronormative moral subjects: Constructing the child and sexual knowledge in schools. *Sexuality and Culture*, 12 (4): 221–239.

Robinson, K. H. & Davies, C. (2010). Tomboys and sissy girls: Exploring girls' power, agency and female relationships in childhood through the memories of women [Special issue]. *Australian Journal of Early Childhood*, 35 (1): 24–31.

Robinson, K. H. & Davies, C. (2015). Children's gendered and sexual cultures: Desiring and regulating recognition through life markers of marriage, love and relationships. In E. Renold, J. Ringrose, & D. R. Egan (Eds.), *Children, Sexuality and Sexualization* (pp. 174–192). London: Palgrave.

Robinson, K. H. & Jones-Diaz, C. (2000). Diversity and difference in early childhood: An investigation into centre policies, staff attitudes and practices. A focus on long day care and preschool in the south west and inner west of Sydney. (December, 2000). Published by Roger A. Baxter, OAS Engineering Pty. Ltd. and The University of Newcastle Research Associates – TUNRA Ltd.

Robinson, K. H. & Jones-Diaz, C. (2006). *Diversity and Difference in Early Childhood: Issues for Theory and Practice*, 1st Edition. Maidenhead: Open University Press.

Robinson, K. H. & Jones-Diaz, C. (2016). *Diversity and Difference in Early Childhood: Issues for Theory and Practice*, 2nd Edition. Maidenhead: Open University Press.

Robinson, K. H., Bansel, P., Denson, N., Ovenden, G., & Davies, C. (2014). *Growing Up Queer: Issues Facing Young Australians Who Are Gender Variant and Sexuality*

Diverse. Melbourne: Young and Well Cooperative Research Centre. ISBN: 978-0-9871179-8-4.

Rose, S. (1999). *Powers of Freedom: Reframing Political Thought*. Cambridge: Cambridge University Press.

Schmitz, S. (2016). The communicative phenomenon of brain-computer-interfaces. In Victoria Pitts-Taylor (Ed.), *Mattering. Feminism, Science, and Materialism*. New York and London: New York University Press.

Schneider, J. (2005). *Donna Haraway: Live Theory*. London: Continuum.

Schwartz, P. & Cappello, D. (2001). *Ten Talks Parents Must Have with Their Children about Sex and Character*. Rydalmere: Hodder Headline Australia.

Sedgwick, E. (1990). *The Epistemology of the Closet*. Berkeley: University of California Press.

Shepherd, L. J. (2014). *Gender Matters in Global Politics: A Feminist Introduction to International Relations*. New York: Routledge, pp. 3–14.

Sirén, J. (2013). *Quest for Bricks*. https://questforbricks.wordpress.com/2013/07/22/on-the-streets-of-billund/accessed 24 July 2016.

Stewart, K. (2007). *Ordinary Affects*. London: Duke University Press.

Stewart, K. (2017). In the World that Affect Proposed. *Cultural Anthropology*, 32 (2): 192–198.

St. Pierre, E. (2017). Writing post qualitative inquiry. *Qualitative Inquiry*. doi: 10.1177/1077800417734567.

St. Pierre, E. & Jackson, A. Y. (2014). Qualitative data analysis after coding. *Qualitative Inquiry*, 20 (6): 715–719.

St. Pierre, E. A., Jackson, A. Y., & Mazzei, L. A. (2016). 'New empiricisms and new materialism: Conditions for new inquiry', *Cultural Studies ↔ Critical Methodologies*,16(2), 111–124.

Stryker, S. (2008). *Transgender History*. Berkeley, CA.: Seal Press.

Taylor, A. (2007). Innocent children, dangerous families and homophobic panic. In G. Morgan & S. Poynting(Eds.), *Outrageous: Moral Panics in Australia*. Hobart: Australian Clearing House for Youth Studies.

Taylor, A. (2013). *Contesting Childhood beyond Nature*. London: Taylor & Francis.

Taylor, A. & Richardson, C. (2005). Queering home corner. *Contemporary Issues in Early Childhood*, 6 (2): 163–173.

Taylor, A., Pacini-Ketchabaw, V., & Blaise, M. (2012). Children's relations to the more-than-human-world [Editorial]. *Contemporary Issues in Early Childhood*, 13 (2): 81–85.

Taylor, C. A. (2013). Objects, bodies and space: Gender and embodied practices of mattering in the classroom. *Gender and Education*, 25 (6): 688–703.

Taylor, C. A. & Hughes, C. (Eds.) (2016). *Posthuman Research Practices in Education*. London: Palgrave Macmillan.

Taylor, C. A. & Ivinson, G. (2013). Material feminisms: New directions for education. *Gender and Education*, 25 (6): 665–670.

Thorne, B. (1993). *Gender Play: Boys and Girls in School*. Buckingham: Open University Press.

Tuana, N. (2008). Viscous porosity: Witnessing Katrina. In S. Alaimo & S. Hekman Eds., *Material Feminisms* (pp. 188–213). Bloomington: Indiana University Press.

Tuck, E. & McKenzie, M. (2015a). *Place in Research: Theory, Methodology, and Methods*. New York: Routledge.

Tuck, E. & McKenzie, M. (2015b). Relational validity and the 'Where' of inquiry: Place and land in qualitative research. *Qualitative Inquiry*: 1–6.

Tynan, L. (2016). Sixty years on, the Maralinga bomb tests remind us not to put security over safety. *The Conversation*, 26 September.

Vallberg Roth, A.-C. (2018). What may characterise teaching in preschool? The written descriptions of Swedish preschool teachers and managers in 2016. *Scandinavian Journal of Educational Research*. doi: 10.1080/00313831.2018.1479301.

Van Der Tuin, I. (2015). *Generational Feminism: New Materialist Introduction to a Generative Approach*. London: Lexington Books.

Walkerdine, V. (1981). Sex, power & pedagogy. *Screen Education*, 38: 14–24.

Walkerdine, V. (1990). *Schoolgirl Fictions*. London: Verson.

West, C. & Zimmerman, D. H. (1987). Doing gender. *Gender and Society*, 1 (2): 125–151.

Whatmore, S. (2006). Materialist returns: Practicing cultural geography in and for a more-than-human world. *Cultural Geography*, 13 (4): 600–809.

Wilson, E. (2004). *Psychosomatic: Feminism and the Neurological Body*. Durham: Duke University Press.

Wolfgang, C. H., Stannard, L. L., & Jones, I. (2001). Block play performance among pre-schoolers as a predictor of later school achievement in mathematics. *Journal of Research in Childhood Education*, Spring–Summer, 2001.

Wulf, C. (2011). Mimesis in early childhood: Enculturation, practical knowledge and performativity. In M. Kontopodis, C. Wulf, & B. Fichtner (Eds.), *Children, Development and Education: Historical, Cultural and Anthropological Perspectives* (pp. 89–99). Dordrecht: Springer.

Young, A. (1990). *Femininity in Dissent*. London: Routledge.

Index